EPIC BUSINESS

30 SECRETS TO BUILD YOUR BUSINESS EXPONENTIALLY AND GIVE YOU THE FREEDOM TO LIVE THE LIFE YOU WANT!

Justin Breen

Epic Business Tag line:
30 Secrets to Build Your Business Exponentially and Give You the
Freedom to Live the Life You Want!

RHG Media Productions
25495 Southwick Drive #103
Hayward, CA 94544.

ISBN 978-1-7348510-0-7 (paperback)

Visit us on line at www.YourPurposeDrivenPractice.com

Printed in the United States of America.

TABLE OF CONTENTS

ACKNOWLEDGEMENTS

To my wife, who has given me a wonderful life
in every way imaginable.

WHAT PEOPLE ARE SAYING...

Justin packs 5,000 watts into this must-read book for anyone who wants to amplify their business or life. Read it now . . . and then—read it again.
~Matt Toledo - CEO, ProVisors

Practical yet personal, Justin Breen's book offers advice that appeals to the common sensibilities of anybody who reads it.
~David Haugh
Longtime Chicago columnist and radio host
670TheScore.com

Chapter by chapter, this book delves into Justin's real-life stories of how his decision-making was influenced, and also fueled, by very particular over-arching principles that every entrepreneur would benefit from.
~Kristin Barnette McCarthy, Trial Attorney at Kralovec, Jambois & Schwartz

Epic Business by Justin Breen is a must-read! He is one of the great geniuses of our time.
~Sarah Victory, Award-winning speaker, best-selling author

If you're interested in becoming an entrepreneur or taking your business to the next level, this is the book to read.
~Jeff Badu, CPA
CEO, Badu Enterprises, LLC

Justin draws you into the book in such a way that, personally, I could not put it down and actually finished it in one day, which is something I never do with non-fiction books of this type.

~Linda F. Patten, Leadership Trainer for Women Entrepreneurs and Changemakers – President &CEO, Dare2Lead With Linda

Epic Business is not just a book on business, it is a book that walks you through the steps of doubling-down on what you are good at while staying true to your passions in life.

~Jeanne Alford, Alford Communications

Epic Business by Justin Breen is a powerful resource that is packed with effective secrets that you can implement immediately.

~Wendy K. Benson, MBA, OTR/L and Elizabeth A. Myers, RN

Co-Authors, The Confident Patient

2x2 Health: Private Health Concierge

Although I have been an entrepreneur myself for 20 years, I picked up some new insights that I could apply in my business.

~Seema Giri, PMP

Award Winning Author, International Speaker, Anthology Compiler and Holistic Lifestyle Strategist

FOREWORD

Becoming a successful negotiator is a lot like building a successful business.

It takes a dedication to learning, loving the journey, empathy, earning a great reputation, and a host of other attributes.

Prior to starting my company—The Black Swan Group—I was the lead international kidnapping negotiator for the Federal Bureau of Investigation, as well as the FBI's hostage negotiation representative for the National Security Council's Hostage Working Group. I also represented the U.S. Government at two international conferences sponsored by the G-8 as an expert in kidnapping negotiations.

Before becoming the FBI lead international kidnapping negotiator, I served as the lead Crisis Negotiator for the New York City Division of the FBI, and I was a member of the New York City Joint Terrorist Task Force for 14 years. I also was the case agent on such cases as TERRSTOP (the Blind Sheikh Case – Sheikh Omar Ali Abdel-Rahman), the TWA Flight 800 catastrophe, and I negotiated the surrender of the first hostage taker to give up in the Chase Manhattan Bank robbery hostage taking. Blah, blah, blah.

The Black Swan Group has more than 10 years of experience working with companies and individuals to take their negotiation skills to the next level. My business teaches you skills that have saved lives and will save deals. Our approach provides specific, actionable skills for navigating the negotiation process.

My book—*Never Split The Difference: Negotiating As If Your Life Depended On It*—detailed what I learned as a negotiator and an entrepreneur.

And many of the lessons mirror what you'll discover in the following pages of *Epic Business*. One of the chapters discusses that you should "never stop learning," something I strongly subscribe to. As my company grows and reaches new audiences, my team and I quest to always get better—to consistently become better businesspeople and negotiators.

Creating the blueprint for a thriving business requires a love of learning, discipline, and dedication. It's all about designing a process that works and then continuing to fine-tune it so it is endlessly improving.

I preach that getting to agreement from a potential client often starts with a "No." I find it wonderful that *Epic Business* discusses the detail of hearing thousands of "No's" that led to agreements with the right people.

Like the success of The Black Swan Group—where I used my years of expertise as a negotiator to build a business that created a groundbreaking model that helps businesses and brands everywhere—BrEpic is doing the same thing with its approach to public relations and building real relationships with a global network.

It's exciting to watch people dream big—and then to actually achieve those dreams!

I hope you enjoy reading this book as much as I did—and learn from its extremely valuable lessons that I think will change the way you look at business . . . and life itself.

Chris Voss
CEO & Founder of The Black Swan Group
Author of *Never Split The Difference: Negotiating As If Your Life Depended On It*

THE BIRTH OF BREPIC

What the f*** am I going to do?

In a five-minute meeting on an early Friday morning – Feb. 10, 2017 – I knew my career as a journalist was over.

In less time than it takes to purchase and pick up a special coffee drink, two decades of climbing the journalism ladder all the way to an amazing Chicago news site was extinguished.

It was a horrible feeling.

I have loved journalism since I was a boy reading the *Chicago Tribune* sports section as a toddler on my father's lap. Being a journalist was all I had ever really wanted to do.

After graduating from the University of Illinois with a degree in News Editorial Journalism, I had several job offers – from Chillicothe, Ohio to Nampa, Idaho – but I chose a sports writing position at the 15,000-circulation *Michigan City News-Dispatch* in Northwest Indiana because it was the closest spot to Chicago – about an hour's drive away. I figured when I started that position in 1999 that I'd be a Chicago reporter within five or six years – at most.

It didn't turn out that way. Slowly but surely, I moved up the ranks – first to the Post-Tribune of Northwest Indiana (60,000 circ.) then to The Times of Northwest Indiana (90,000) – before finally landing a position at DNAinfo

Chicago – a startup news site that had launched in New York City and was expanding to Chicago in 2012.

After a rigorous interview process that lasted several months, I received a phone call that I had been hired as a Senior Editor at the site. After failed interviews with the *Tribune*, *Sun-Times*, *Crain's Chicago Business*, *Daily Herald*, Associated Press' Chicago Bureau and numerous other Chicago-area publications in the previous decade-plus, I had finally made it to the big time.

For those who don't know what DNAinfo Chicago was, it was a journalism Valhalla. Our fearless staff of awesome reporters and editors for the most part got to write and cover the stories we wanted to – fun stuff, interesting stuff, very neighborhood focused to the street corners. There were efforts to *grow* the business, build a name, a big following, take the model to other cities around the country.

It was super exciting.

And then it all hit the fan.

On a Thursday afternoon, I received an email from our managing editor that I needed to come to the office early Friday morning. I knew that wasn't a good sign as Fridays were usually my writing days and I never went to the office.

The next day, after running on Northerly Island as the sun rose, I entered the office and sat down with the managing editor and the site's owner. It was explained that due to cost cuts, I was being demoted to a reporter position and my salary was essentially being cut in half. A few other folks had their positions terminated, so in a way I felt blessed to still have a job and some salary.

But I knew journalism was done.

And I had to figure something else out – and soon.

So I did what most others do – scrambled to find a full-time job. And as those who are trying to find jobs know rather well, it's a black hole applying for positions. It's a nightmare. Demoralizing. A total mind suck.

Over the next month or so, I reached out to my thousands of contacts that I had built over the years and basically begged them for help. I had bills to pay. My family lives in the North Shore of Chicago – it's not cheap to set up shop here.

A few breaks led to some freelance work running social media sites and pitching stories to keep me afloat while I also worked full-time as a DNAinfo Chicago reporter. It was the equivalent of clocking 80 hours a week to pay for the same 40-hour salary I had made as an editor.

On April 6, 2017, my wonderful wife, Sarah, surprised me with a trip to Kohler, Wisconsin, for my 40th birthday – which was four days later. Devastated with the job search but somewhat excited about my freelance opportunities, it popped into my head to just go for it and start my own thing. Just after passing the Bong Recreation Area sign heading north on Interstate 94 in southern Wisconsin, the name "BrEpic" came out of my mouth as the name for the company.

It's a ridiculous name – Br for the first two letters of my last name; Epic because, frankly, I just use the word constantly in stories, in conversation and on social media – but I thought it would be really catchy, too, because people are always saying Epic as well.

On April 16, I officially incorporated and spent the next six weeks reaching out to 5,000-plus people to land BrEpic's first five clients. I told myself that when I hit the five-client threshold, I would resign from DNAinfo. The goal was hit on June 1, I resigned June 2 and officially announced BrEpic's arrival on June 5 through a great story by top media journalist Robert Feder.

And what an epic ride it has been since.....
****

So what's the point of this book? Why should you care? I'm just another guy who got kicked in the gut and turned his life around, right?

Wrong. I discovered the 30 real-life secrets to help you achieve your dreams, make more money than you ever have before, spend more time with your family and friends, and work with the people, businesses and brands that you *want* to.

I absolutely know the 30 secrets in this book will *help* you in endless ways. If you follow and implement these tips that I've learned from listening to some of the world's best and brightest visionary entrepreneurs, business leaders and just great people out there, your life should dramatically change.

For those who are entrepreneurs or hopeful entrepreneurs, I'm going to go into a great deal of the exhilarating, excruciating, deflating, inspirational, mind-blowing, you-can-jump-out-of-a-plane ride that this life has to offer. I am holding nothing back – except not revealing some people's full names to protect their identities – because followings see the highs but most don't fully understand the lows.

This list of 30 things I've learned was built over my years as an entrepreneur and was originally meant for a social media post to inspire others. But so many high-level folks told me it should be a book – and others even printed out the list and brought it to our meetings as a surprise – that I knew it was much bigger than just a conversation starter on LinkedIn and Facebook.

With the help of countless others and using these 30 tips, I have built an international business working with some of the most amazing visionary people in the world.

All I want is for others to achieve this kind of success – and have this kind of incredible joy in their lives.

LINK:

https://www.robertfeder.com/2017/06/05/robservations-justin-breen-leaves-dnainfo-new-adventure/

CHAPTER ONE
PRIORITIZE FAMILY TIME OVER WORK TIME

If you are someone who believes that family shouldn't come first, please put down the book. I can't help you.

BrEpic has been successful in large part because I spend *more* time with my family than I did when I was a full-time journalist. I work *less* than I ever have before. If it's clear that a potential client would cause problems and result in less quality time with my wife and children, there is zero chance I would sign with them.

It's important to explain why I feel this way and how my life has been shaped by two critical moments – the deaths of my father, Mike, and youngest brother, Jerry.

My dad was 61 years old when I was born. He was a World War II First Lieutenant who fought Nazis in Belgium's and Germany's Hürtgen Forest, climbed mountains covered with ice, flew in bomber planes dealing with enemy fire, was an attorney in the Nuremberg Trials, was president of a major insurance company and was loved by all. I never heard anyone say a bad word about him – ever.

He was the greatest father imaginable. Despite his age, he played basketball, baseball and other sports with me and my two younger brothers. He was partially retired during our childhood, so he was home a lot. We spent tons of time at Arlington International Racetrack, too, betting on the ponies. We watched R-rated movies like *Robocop*, *48 Hours* and *Platoon*. For me, it just seemed like a normal childhood. He was my hero in every way.

So when I was pulled out of an eighth-grade morning class on Monday, Jan. 14, 1991 – when I was 13 years old – I didn't think much of it until I asked the assistant principal what was wrong, and he didn't say anything other than a neighbor was going to pick me up and tell me more. My friend's mother from across the street ushered me into a backseat in her car and drove me to Glenbrook Hospital's emergency room about 10 minutes away. She said something had happened to my dad.

I walked into the ER with my brothers and was told to come to a room, where they opened the door and my father was lying with a gown – he had defecated, and the smell was apparent – with tubes and needles inserted all over his body. He was still awake and softly uttered "my boys!" – he always said that when he came home – before my brothers and I got to briefly hug him and tell him I loved him. That was the last time I saw my father – he died Jan. 18. He fell victim to a fatal heart attack, and I strongly believed he used his last moments of consciousness to say goodbye to his children.

For a 13-year-old boy who in a few months was about to enter high school, I can't imagine anything worse than losing your father and best friend. The memory of him in the hospital – seeing my idol helpless on an operating table bed – is so built into my fabric that I know it will never be erased. It probably doesn't help that I live a few blocks from this hospital and run past it six times a week during my morning exercise routine.

With my own sons – Jake, 7, and Chase, 5, at the time of this writing – I treat them very similarly to how my dad acted with me: fun, almost childlike. I actively play with them at school – where I'm the only dad on the PTO – while most other parents talk amongst themselves. We go to see R-rated movies. We have the best time, and I also always make sure they order for themselves, and say "please" and "thank you." And if I ever see anyone in military uniform, I always tell them that that person is a hero and they should be very thankful they are serving our country.

My father's death denied me the childhood and early adulthood I deserved, and I won't deny my kids the same opportunity.

My youngest brother, Jerry, tried to jump into my father's grave when they lowered him into the ground. I don't think he ever recovered from my dad's death. He was only 10 at the time.

Jerry and I didn't have a great relationship, but he was still my youngest brother, and he was a genius – a brilliant piano and guitar player who could jam without ever reading music.

Jerry was a free spirit who went to numerous colleges. He was working on his Ph.D. at the University of Central Florida in his final years, when he also was one of the many victims of this nation's opioid crisis.

On Saturday, March 27, 2010, I was Sports Editor at The Times of Northwest Indiana, and we had three boys basketball teams competing in the Indiana state championship games. We deployed a full reporting staff to the games in Indianapolis, and I was in charge of overseeing a giant special section with bundles of stories, photos, graphics and more. Typical hours as a sports editor on a Saturday were from 2 p.m. to midnight, but I stayed at the office until well past 2 a.m. that shift and was extremely proud of the section the staff created on tight deadline.

Still buzzing off the accomplishment, I slept very little that night but was awoken that morning with a call from my mom, who said my brother had died and that he was found by police deceased in the hotel room where he was residing.

Jerry was 29 years old. He never got to meet my children.

Immediately, I realized that work accomplishments amounted to very little in life. The thought of my brother lying dead alone in a hotel room while I was celebrating a silly basketball special section was the ultimate reality check.

I had been consumed with professional success until that moment but understood after that 20-second phone call that life was short, and I needed to make the most of it. I apply that to my family, business, friends and elsewhere.

I hope it doesn't take tragedies to make you realize the importance of family before everything else. When I meet successful entrepreneurs, I always ask them how much time they spent with their families. It pains me when I talk to the folks who have made millions, and they respond they that wish they had experienced more time with their families and the regrets they have because of it. There are others who said they put everything into work and thus never had families. That's a real tragedy.

It has worked out that most of my company's clients put family first. I can't tell you how many of my clients have told me that they started a business mainly so they could be with their families more – when they wanted to.

And guess what? Those clients who put family first have great relationships with the same type of amazing business owners. And that many times leads to more and more business with the *right* groups of people.

Even in the first six months of BrEpic, when it was a struggle to find business and attract the right types of folks, I would routinely ask myself the same question after meeting with a potential client: **Is this person or business going to cause unnecessary stress or problems that will disrupt quality time with my family?**

If the answer was definitely "yes," I would not work with the prospective client and just move on. In BrEpic's beginning stages, if the response in my head was "maybe," I would sign a contract, but after the six-month mark of the company, there's simply no way I would do it.

For the most part, I've weeded out potential bad clients – we'll get to that in the coming chapters – but the simple question above is a perfect barometer to quickly trim the fat of a potential nudnik.

When I meet and talk to a potential client, work is never brought up first. It's always family. I speak about raising two wild sons. I tell them about how my wife and I were featured on *The Today Show*, in the *Chicago Tribune* and numerous other media outlets for going out on dates once a week for 52 straight weeks without our children in 2018. It's a great way to inspire people that you can have an awesome life by prioritizing family while still doing amazing work for clients.

For me, it's the only way.

EPIC TAKEAWAYS:

1. Shift to put your family first
2. Be mindful of what you are saying yes or no to
3. Align your work, time and energy with what is most important to you

LINK:

http://52dates52weeks.com/

CHAPTER TWO

DO WHAT YOU LOVE TO DO AND WHAT YOU DO BEST

In the first few months of BrEpic, if a potential client asked me to jump, I would respond, *how high?*

Keep in mind, I had no idea *how* to run a business. I took zero business classes in college. I didn't know what a W-9 was or what LLC stood for until I decided to create BrEpic. There had been no reason to learn any of this while working in the corporate world.

During BrEpic's initial quarters, I ran social media accounts, created press releases – anything that clients requested, I would do. Occasionally, though, I was able to interject and request to write actual *stories* for clients, and I would pitch those stories to mainstream media. These were *not* press releases; they were more like articles complete with a headline, photos and even embedded videos.

They were very similar to the stories I was writing and had written at DNAinfo Chicago and other journalism stops during my two-decade professional career. And when I was at DNAinfo, many times I would get a scoop or exclusive and then pitch that story link to the competition like TV, radio stations, and bigger online and print publications, because I hoped to see "as first reported in DNAinfo Chicago" somewhere in those stories. It was great publicity for our news site that had built a great following but was always looking for more readership or notoriety.

When I was pitching these stories – again, not press releases – for clients, I noticed the success rate of getting picked up by outlets was staggeringly high. Media *wanted* this type of content and was appreciative for me sending it their way. It was the opposite of receiving a press release – as a journalist, you get hundreds of these ridiculously bad emails every day, and it burns bridges and flat-out annoys you.

It was thrilling to see my clients earning major mainstream media hits, and it was fun to write these stories that were actually interesting and served the *journalist*, not the business. I thought there was enough there to solely base my entire business on the process of writing and pitching these stories. I love doing it, and I'm really good at it, too.

That was cemented when, a few months into BrEpic, I had drinks with a super successful entrepreneur, Edward, who has appeared on numerous national hit television shows and is a major player in tech sales. He asked what BrEpic's business model consisted of, and I told him it included running social media and creating those awful press releases, but also the writing/pitching of these super cool stories that were almost exactly like journalistic articles.

The single most important thing I've learned and implemented since starting BrEpic is when Edward shared with me that the top entrepreneurs he knows *always focus on one key business plan and continue to double down on it*.

I absorbed this ultra-important lesson and did not renew any contracts that didn't focus solely on crafting great stories and pitching those stories to media. Over the next few months, my sales pitch to potential new clients highlighted only the writing and pitching of stories. BrEpic's website changed to showcase this simple process of building business' brands and identities by getting their stories out to media. When I gave interviews with mainstream media about BrEpic, it was solely to focus on this process.

I can't tell you how many times a potential client has told me that when they talk to other PR firms, they don't know what that firm does. I never really understood it either. But my business model and process are so streamlined, that even a grade-schooler can break it down. **BrEpic creates newsworthy stories and pitches those stories to media.** That's it.

Simple.

Effective.

And fun for me.

The model works for any size business in any vertical in any market. It's the *model* that works; it doesn't matter what the business is or where it's located.

I've continued to double down on the business – adding freelance reporters, a website producer and a virtual assistant (we'll get to that more in Chapter 24) – while continuing to focus on my core strengths.

In late 2018, I wrote a story for one of my university clients about one of its star graduates, Scott, a titan in the law, medical and media fields. During the interview, I told him about why BrEpic had quickly become successful due to its focus on core strengths, and I could tell Scott was in total agreement. He followed by saying that he "learned how important it was to focus on our core areas, and we've consistently doubled down in those areas to grow around our core."

My core has been molded and enhanced into what numerous high-level groups call someone's "Unique Ability."

My latest version of Unique Ability – as I'm sure it will evolve in the coming years – is the following:

"I am hard-wired to seek out and create viral, thought-provoking stories that the media craves. And I find the best stories when I network with visionary entrepreneurs and executives who understand the value of investing in themselves and their businesses."

As BrEpic continues to grow, I will spend more time on enhancing my Unique Ability and less time on everything else.

I will never get bored or tired of writing these stories and connecting with amazing entrepreneurs and executives.

Because when you focus on what you love doing and what you're truly good at, it never feels like "working."

EPIC TAKEAWAYS:

1. Simplify and streamline your focus to align with your unique ability
2. What can you stop doing or take off your plate as it doesn't align with your unique ability?
3. Check in and do more of what you love doing and are good at. This will never feel like "work"

CHAPTER THREE
WORK WITH PEOPLE WHO VIEW PARTNERSHIPS AS INVESTMENTS, NOT COSTS

When someone asks "*How much does this cost?*" it's almost a certain dead giveaway they won't be able to afford you or won't be a good client.

I can't recall one person who posed this question within the first five minutes of our meeting that became a client. If that's the question lingering in someone's head, my experience is that they'll only be thinking about cost – instead of *investment* – during the entire partnership.

Looking at the pure definition of cost and investment to me is very revealing.

A cost is "an amount that has to be paid or spent to buy or obtain something."

An investment, according to the Oxford Dictionary, is: "the action or process of investing money for profit or material result."

BrEpic's earliest clients were extremely hesitant and tentative to spend their money because, to them, everything is their businesses was looked at as a "cost." They were far more worried about the expense of a project than what the obvious gains could be – like more media exposure, more people providing donations, and gaining validity and credibility from potential customers. They weren't visionaries. Everything was in the moment, getting through the next business cycle or paying the bills. Scattered and edgy.

And what was *really* interesting was that, for the most part, the clients' personalities reflected this dread of spending. They were quick to criticize and judge and almost never provided compliments. I couldn't get into their heads, but they didn't seem like happy people in general. I know BrEpic provides tremendous value for its clients and was always a little surprised that many clients weren't appreciative of their appearing in major mainstream media throughout the world, and how it helped them.

As I raised BrEpic's rates (see Chapter 9), I started to weed almost all of these businesses and brands out.

The "cost" question started to be heard less and less. Instead, potential clients began asking things like *"what does an investment with your business look like?"* They realized what mainstream media publicity could do for them and their businesses. How it could attract speaking engagements or new clients or help improve their closing rate with potential customers.

These are the folks who dreamed big – and actually were achieving those dreams. I've had clients take out loans to pay for BrEpic's services; others have ordered an additional credit card to invest with my firm. And they've easily 10X'd those investments. They understood the definition of investment to obtain "profit or material result." Successful media campaigns have literally changed their lives, and they envisioned it!

And because they were living their dreams and investing with BrEpic to help make that happen, almost all these clients were extremely happy. There has been almost no nitpicking; instead they are all appreciative and say thank you consistently, for any type of media interview – no matter how big or small. They are having *fun* with the process of arranging and conducting interviews with media. Many of my firm's clients tell me that earning mainstream media results is the best part of their day or week because they're getting to share their interesting stories with the world – and building their businesses in the process.

Recently, I had a call with a potential client where he began the conversation like this: *"Justin, I'm really excited to talk to you. Numerous people have told me how investing with your company has helped their businesses. What does a typical investment with you look like?"*

These are the types of conversations you want to have with the people you want to do business with.

Hearing the word "cost" is almost never a good sign.

But when someone utters "investment," it should be music to your ears.

EPIC TAKEAWAYS:

1. What language is your potential client using? Cost or Investment?
2. What language are you using? Cost or Investment?
3. How can you shift to talking more about investing versus cost?

CHAPTER FOUR

YOUR CLIENTS BECOME YOUR FRIENDS, AND YOUR FRIENDS BECOME YOUR CLIENTS

Almost all of my friends are entrepreneurs.

I'm so passionate about building a business and working with visionaries, that I don't really have much to talk about with people who don't think the same way.

The people I am closest with outside of family *only think big* like me. Dan Sullivan, the founder of the best networking group I'm in, Strategic Coach (Chapter 15), said that's crucial. In a post titled "Why it matters who you hang out with," Sullivan wrote: **"The opinions of our close friends and associates will always carry importance. They will always be a factor in how we plan our futures, what goals we set, and how we plan to take action on them."**

My best friend, Chris, is an entrepreneur who sold his first company and is starting a second. He became my client as well to promote his newest company. For the last two-plus years since I've launched my business, we've talked almost every weekday.

He knows everything I've been through since founding BrEpic; I know everything he's endured since selling his company, which took more than a year, and creating another one.

The entrepreneurial world can be *extremely* lonely. *Forbes* in 2018 noted that "isolation was cited as one of the biggest challenges faced by business owners and sole traders." Loneliness, the publication stressed, "leads to depression, stress, anxiety and can cause a range of mental illnesses."

I can't tell you how great it is to have friends who understand what you're going through. Inc reported in 2018 that the United States is filled with 27 million entrepreneurs – or 14 percent of the population – but most of them are running super small businesses with no aspirations to become visionaries or make their businesses brand names on an international level. Businesses like painters, mom-and-pop stores and tiny restaurants almost certainly won't become my firm's clients because they almost certainly think first of expenses and costs, not investments.

So the pool of potential clients is a bit smaller for people like me. And **when I find folks who have the same go-for-it, no-BS attitude, I can *talk to them for hours*! It is infectious hanging out with people like that. Because they get it!**

And these are the ones who become my friends and very possibly my clients.

Late in 2019, I was referred to a sales entrepreneur named Kyle. He and I first spoke on the phone, immediately bonded and set up an in-person meeting. He could see I was serious and immediately began thinking of people to introduce me to. I did the same for him.

Later that night, he sent an intro email that in part read "*copied Justin Breen who I just met today. He is ONE of us, fear not! Gotta meet the guy.*" I have no doubt that Kyle will become my friend and a great referral source for years to come because he and I are on the same page. I wouldn't be surprised if his business eventually became my firm's client as well.

Clients routinely invite me to their private parties; one just took my wife and me on a pizza tour of Chicago. We went to dinner and a comedy show with another client and her spouse.

Friends are great referral sources, too. One my fraternity brothers, Rob, referred me to the communications director at his national IT company, and they became a long-term client. A friend referred me to the marketing director of a medical practice in Wisconsin that signed an incredible contract. A friend and fellow entrepreneur referred me to a thriving self-storage business that turned into a great partnership. I helped a friend start her own business, and then she became a client.

The bottom line here is that between visionary-thinking entrepreneurs, there is a tremendous amount of respect and admiration for one another. Those relationships and common bonds lead to friendship and very possibly doing business together.

EPIC TAKEAWAYS:

1. Pay attention to who you surround yourself with. Are they on a similar journey?
2. How can you cheer each other on and then go deeper?
3. Who are amazing people you can introduce your amazing people to?

LINKS:

https://resources.strategiccoach.com/the-multiplier-mindset-blog/why-it-matters-who-you-hang-out-with

https://www.inc.com/leigh-buchanan/us-entrepreneurship-reaches-record-highs.html

CHAPTER FIVE

WHEN YOU START A BUSINESS, IT TAKES TWO FULL YEARS TO REALLY FIGURE THINGS OUT

BrEpic – thank God – for the most part has been very financially successful from the start.

But just because I was making money as a business owner – way more than I ever had as a journalist – didn't mean I understood my target market, my core customer, my process, my network, my pricing structure or pretty much anything else.

A lot of the successes my firm has had is because I threw stuff against a wall, and some of it stuck while a lot of it led to huge failures.

A good friend of mine is a high-powered, very successful attorney named Kristin. When I was a journalist, I interviewed her for a story, and she quickly became my buddy. Since the start of BrEpic, I've met with her at a downtown Chicago coffee shop about once every other month. She is involved with numerous exclusive boards and organizations, and knows what she is talking about.

So during BrEpic's early days when Kristin and I were talking over breakfast, I told her about the chaos – the ups and downs – of the company even though it was making tremendous money.

She stopped me, nicely, and said **"don't worry, when you start a business, it takes two years to really figure it out."**

As a journalist, it's go-go-go-go, deadline-deadline-deadline-deadline, next story-next story-next story-next story *all ... the ... time.* **But in business, it's just not like that. It's a much sssslllllloooowwwweeeerrrr pace. Things just take time.**

But I didn't know that in the first few months of BrEpic. And even though I had a process of writing and pitching stories quite refined, there were numerous other tweaks to go. Even though I was receiving decent referrals, most were still not for the right group of people – the visionary people I almost exclusively work with now.

I also wasn't in the right networking groups yet. My rates weren't high enough to weed out the nonsense. I didn't understand that contracts sometimes take months – if not years – to actually get signed. My website wasn't that great – at that point, I was still updating it myself and not working with an expert in the field.

As BrEpic has slowly but surely built its foundation and found the right fits, the right people and the right brands to do business with, Kristin's statement has always kept me grounded. I needed to hear and understand what she said because otherwise I would feel like a hamster routinely stuck on a never-stopping wheel, or a 4x4 endlessly spinning its tires.

The two-year, longer-term vision was so crucial to stay focused but also to realize that running a business would not be an overnight sensation – that *years* would be required for it to really get it humming.

On BrEpic's two-year anniversary in April of 2019, my wife and I went back to Kohler, Wisconsin to celebrate the company's growth. We went to the same five-star restaurant that we dined at in 2017; it was the first time I ate Wagyu A5 beef, and oh my God is that good.

As my wife and I talked about our children and the company – among other things – I realized how Kristin's words more than 18 months earlier were so true.

By that dinner, I had begun dealing with almost only high-level clients. The process of creating stories and pitching them to media was seamless, and I had started to add freelance reporters to my team. I hired a website designer to build a beautiful site filled with videos, photos, a graphic showing BrEpic's plan to help potential clients, great referral quotes from clients and other fun items.

My networking groups were the *right* fit. Clients were becoming friends, and friends were becoming clients. Visionaries were referring me to other visionaries, across the country and world. I was ready to start thinking about the business five, 10, even 20 years from now.

My rates had gone *way* up. My sales pitch to customers was very direct. Only the cream of the crop – my dad always told me the cream always rose to the top – type of folks were signing. And that's what I wanted.

Contracts that had been discussed in 2018 were getting signed in 2019. Meetings I had in 2017 were leading to referrals. Business was really booming, and it kept getting *better and better.*

Probably 2-3 times a month, people who have just started a business or are about to start one ask me for pointers. When I talk on the phone or meet with them, it's obvious they have this sense of excitement but also absolute dread. They have no clue what type of roller coaster awaits them.

They usually say they're inspired by BrEpic's growth, and I always tell them, thanks, but they didn't see me when I was up at 3 a.m. with almost zero clients in a full-blown panic sweating thinking what the hell did I just do with my life!

Like Kristin tried to calm me down and give me perspective, I attempt to do the same for new business owners. The recently baptized entrepreneurs usually spend about 4-5 minutes discussing what they're doing, why they want to do it, and essentially that they don't know how the bleep they're going to accomplish any of it.

So I follow by saying, relax, it's going to be OK – and realize that it will take time to figure it out. Not weeks, not months, but *years*. Two years in fact.

And when I say that, it's almost always followed by my conversation mate taking a deep breath and then smiling. I can tell what a relief it is for them to hear that, and that they don't have to have all the answers right now or even within a year.

Besides doing what you love to do and what you're good at, Kristin's advice that it takes two years to really figure things out has been the most important lesson I've learned since founding BrEpic. I am so thankful to Kristin for changing my mindset with one forever-memorable sentence.

EPIC TAKEAWAYS:

1. It's OK to give yourself time to figure it out
2. Find the right networking groups for you
3. Give others time to figure it out, too
4. Encourage others along the way reminding them it's OK to take time to figure it out, too

CHAPTER SIX
NEVER STOP LEARNING

Most of the entrepreneurs I know are voracious readers. Some read hundreds of pages a day. They *love* learning.

I can't think of one super successful person in my giant network who stays stagnant or doesn't want to constantly learn more, more, more and more.

One of my clients, Larry, who started his fractional CFO business in his 60s and is now in his early 70s, has an absolute zest for discovering new ideas and tactics every day. It's always refreshing to see him because he has such a craving for knowledge and how he can use that to help people and build his business.

This book represents what I've learned from talking to some of the best, most innovative and brilliant people on the planet. I am in a constant quest to find these types of visionaries because they have so much to share – **and they want to share as they always have a "give first" attitude.**

Inc, Business Insider and numerous other publications noted how Warren Buffett reads as many as 1,000 pages of a book every day. He said that's been a big reason why he's had success – by using the knowledge he's absorbed through reading and then using it to make informed, thoughtful decisions. **Those articles also stress that Buffett spends as much as 80 percent of his day reading magazines, periodicals, newspapers and other publications.**

Learning to me doesn't mean studying or taking adult-level classes after college or anything like that. I was an above-average student and scored a 32 on the ACT, but I didn't have a passion for educational books, formulas or that kind of thing.

To me, learning is stimulating your mind by meeting incredible people and implementing their lessons. And it's about reading fascinating articles and nonfiction books. I routinely post on social media asking my followers to send me great nonfiction book recommendations, and it's always so cool to see their responses because 1. People are still reading at a massive level; and 2. It's great to receive such a plethora of options on every type of topic imaginable. Over the past decade or so, I've built up a pretty neat list of nonfiction literature, and if you'd like me to send it to you, please email me at Justin@BrEpicLLC.com.

My goal is to learn at least one really profound thing every day. I keep track of it on an awesome free app called Win Streak. I highly recommend that you utilize it. It's a super simple way of logging great events or lessons learned, and it's very helpful in allowing you to scan the previous days, weeks and months.

Numerous data have shown that people who fill their minds with new knowledge are happier than those who don't. Countless articles, like this Inc piece, detail how rich people usually watch an hour or less television each day, while most poor people veg out in front of the tube for at least two hours a day. Don't get me wrong, I love TV – especially live sports – but I'd rather read a good nonfiction book that teaches me something about an event, faraway land, group of people I've never heard of, or a policy that has shaped how we run our lives.

My father in his 70s would play Scrabble against himself for hours in the living room. As a child, I never understood why he was doing that, but now that I'm older, I'm pretty sure it's because he wanted to challenge his brain to turn jumbled letters into complicated words.

I'm glad I share his joy of words – and learning.

EPIC TAKEAWAYS:

1. Develop a love of learning
2. Visionaries have a give-first attitude
3. Read more to grow and learn
4. Set a "learning goal" each day or week
5. Track your epic ideas, thoughts and lessons learned

LINKS:

https://www.inc.com/marcel-schwantes/warren-buffett-says-anyone-can-achieve-success-if-they-follow-1-simple-rule-he-calls-the-buffett-formula.html

https://www.inc.com/marissa-levin/reading-habits-of-the-most-successful-leaders-that.html

CHAPTER SEVEN

YOUR NETWORK EQUALS YOUR NET WORTH

One of my business friends, Quinton, says this phrase every time he speaks to a group. I've probably heard him utter "Your network equals your net worth" 150 times – if not more.

When I was a journalist, well over half of my stories came from scrolling my Twitter feed – which is filled with more than 10,000 contacts – and finding things I found interesting. My social network was crucial to discovering great content to share with readers.

When I started BrEpic, my network was even more important when trying to find freelance or contract opportunities. I routinely tell people that I reached out to 5,000 people to land BrEpic's first five clients, but it was likely *way* more than 5,000. If I didn't have that network, which had been built over 20 years of being a journalist, starting a business would have been almost impossible.

I have about 37,000 followers on social media – including more than 17,000 on LinkedIn. Social media posts have led to tens of thousands of dollars in contracts for my firm. I post fun, organic things that highlight my firm's clients or BrEpic itself. When you create authentic content, it can lead to huge results.

My favorite social media story involves McDonald's and the No. 2 Extra Value Meal. I love McDonald's, and so do my sons. My favorite meal was the No. 2 Extra Value Meal, which consisted of two cheeseburgers, fries and a drink. I had ordered it for decades.

A few years ago, McDonald's took the meal off the menu. I tried ordering it, and the employee at the register said I couldn't get it anymore. I was upset – not really upset, but jokingly upset. So I sent a silly tweet to McDonald's noting how could they have the audacity to remove my go-to meal from the menu.

Fast forward six months, and of course I had completely forgotten about the tweet. But McDonald's hadn't! They replied to my original tweet saying they had heard my complaint and put the two-cheeseburger meal *back on the menu!* It was the No. 9 Meal now, but who cared!

I created a screen-grab of the McDonald's tweet and posted it on social media. Reaction was crazy! Everyone was liking it, but the best part was one of my Facebook friends said she loved the effort, and her company wanted to work with my firm. And that led to a *five-figure contract!!!*

Your network equals your net worth.

Social media is just one component – although a very important component – of a network. I'll dive into more detail on networking groups in Chapter 15, but spending quality time actually networking in person with the right people is beyond essential.

And being involved in the right organizations is vital as well. For more than a decade, I've been Journalism Chair for the University of Illinois College of Media Alumni Board. It's a long title that means I help the college's journalism program run events and assists students and recent graduates in finding jobs. I just enjoy assisting the college and the students/ alumni, but the position has led to a wealth of opportunities.

For one, there are U of I graduates in virtually every media market in the United States. So when I pitch stories, it's easy to find folks I know in cities big and small.

It's also led to financial gain. One of the College of Media's top officials a few years ago moved to a similar position at a different college within the University of Illinois. I've been friends with this person for a decade. So when the college where this person now worked at needed help earning mainstream media publicity, guess with whom they connected? And that led to a giant contract publicizing some truly incredible students and graduates at the college.

When you find the right network and build it with the right people, it will only lead to more of the same right-fit opportunities. In terms of working "in" the business, I spend the most percentage of my time networking – either on social media, on the phone, in person or within groups. Again, it's included in my Unique Ability – ... *I find the best stories when I network with visionary entrepreneurs and executives who understand the value of investing in themselves and their businesses* – so it's part of my fabric in terms of what I really care about, and what I really do best.

And I also maintain and support my network by becoming a trusted, go-to resource by connecting people within my web. I create daily connections within my network, and, trust me, this is extremely powerful and has endless benefits for my clients, business partners and myself.

People ask me all the time how I built a business working with all these amazing people and brands. And I tell them it's because of my network. That's really what BrEpic is – a company promoting an incredible network of visionary entrepreneurs to the world!

It's all about understanding that simple phrase: *Your network equals your net worth.*

EPIC TAKEAWAYS:

1. Who is in your network?
2. How are you building and maintaining your network?
3. How do you share successes and connections with your network?
4. Never underestimate the impact your message and shares can make in media and your network
5. Be willing to make thoughtful connections/introductions to and with your network
6. Be a trusted resource for others
7. Become a "go to connector" (People know they can come to you and you can introduce them to that right person for their need.)
8. People like to do business with people they like, know and trust
9. Celebrate your successes and the successes of those in your network

IF YOU THINK OF YOURSELF AS NICKEL AND DIME, YOU WILL ALWAYS BE NICKEL AND DIME. INSTEAD, CHOOSE TO VALUE YOURSELF.

I'm amazed that so many people don't value *themselves* and their worth.

The strict Oxford Dictionary definition of "nickel and dime" as a verb is to "put a financial strain on (someone) by charging small amounts for many minor services." As an adjective, nickel and dime is defined as "of little importance; petty."

So why would anyone think of themselves like that?

Since starting my business, I've discovered this simple truth: Nickel and dime people hang out with other nickel and dime people. Whether that's in social settings, networking groups or online, they stick together.

And trust me, you don't want any part of it.

From my experience, nickel and dime people are TOXIC for a few key reasons: 1. They can't afford what you do; 2. If they do sign, they are going to question every decision you make;

and 3. They will refer you to other nickel and dime people because those are the only types of people in their networks.

When I was in the wrong networking groups, I met a lot of nickel and dime people. **They had businesses that were going nowhere, working with clients for teeny-tiny fees and had no vision for long-term growth.** I felt like an alien attending these meetings and after a few weeks realized there was zero chance I could benefit socially, mentally, financially or any other way by continuing to go. So I stopped.

I'll save you the trouble by providing a few ways to identify nickel and dime people so you don't have to go through the same brain-drain, time-waste nonsense I did.

1. Nickel and dime people usually charge by the hour. With the exception of attorneys, who are bound by a business model for the most part to charge hourly, potential clients who say they work on an hourly fee should be avoided like the plague.
2. Nickel and dime people love working with only super small businesses. If you ask someone who their clients are, and they say they have a soft spot for working with the underdog or only minute, neighborhood companies, they are likely nickel and dime.
3. If someone is constantly complaining about their business or their clients, they are almost certainly nickel and dime.
4. If you tell someone your rates and they look like they are going to have a stroke, they are nickel and dime.

I read a lot of publications and when there's an article about someone interesting who could be a good partner for my firm, I routinely reach out via social media. That was the case in mid-2019 when I came across an interesting article on a CEO marketing whiz named Chris. He was helping a lot of cool companies and had a vision to make his company great. His corporate past included leadership roles at major brands like PetSmart, US Cellular and AT&T. This dude knew what he was doing.

So I sent him a message on LinkedIn and he immediately responded. I could tell from our back-and-forth messaging that he was *not* nickel and dime. We set up a time to talk on the phone, and proceeded to have a great, hour-long conversation.

In that 60-minute talk, a few bullet points stood out. Chris had a strong vision for growth, but he was currently working with too many nickel and dime clients. He was charging by the hour for numerous clients, many of which were super-small businesses. But he did not want to work with those businesses any longer because, like I said, he was not nickel and dime.

I told him what I tell a lot of folks struggling with the nickel and dime mindset. First, I stressed he had to immediately double or even triple his rates to weed out the smallest clients. Second, I recommended he join some of my networking groups, and I'd be happy to set up introductory emails to my contacts. We met in person a few weeks later, and he was ready for the intros and to start raising his rates.

A few months after that, I ran into him during a holiday party at a swank Downtown Chicago social club for one of my high-level networking groups. He had a big *smile* on his face. After saying hello, he immediately blurted out that almost all of his nickel and dime clients were gone because he had substantially raised his rates, and he had almost completely stopped charging by the hour – instead he was charging by the project. And he exclaimed that the networking group I had introduced him to had led him to meeting the right types of potential clients. In this particular group, almost no one thinks of themselves as nickel and dime. It creates a great culture and a ton of business opportunities for everyone.

When you value yourself and your worth, it attracts other people who value themselves and their worth. Nickel and dimers magnetize other nickel and dimers. Visionaries flock to other visionaries.

I hope that, as you read this, if you currently think of yourself as nickel and dime, that you can seriously start to change that mentality. It might take a bit, but the long-term benefits are endless!

EPIC TAKEAWAYS:

1. Check in...Are you getting caught up in the nickel and dime mentality?
2. Are you hanging out with and networking with nickel and dime people?
3. Be willing to value yourself, your services, and your results and shift to a visionary mindset and approach
4. Adjust your rates accordingly
5. Network and hang out with other visionary experts

LINK:

https://www.lexico.com/en/definition/nickel-and-dime

RAISING YOUR RATES EARNS YOU RESPECT FROM THE PEOPLE AND CLIENTS THAT MATTER THE MOST

Starting a business is all about taking a leap of faith. The next leap many times consists of raising your rates.

People ask me frequently when BrEpic really started to take off. And I tell them that the main factor is when I *tripled* – and even *quadrupled* my rates!

In PR, nothing is guaranteed – if a PR firm promises you something, I strongly suggest not working with them – but I occasionally will ask clients for their Return On Investment. For example, I'll request they send me how mainstream media articles led to them earning new clients, leads, speaking opportunities or other financial gain. And what I found was that every time I asked, the clients were earning huge ROIs – far larger returns than what BrEpic's rates were.

This was reinforced when I met with an executive of a giant PR company and their minimum rates to work with anyone were well into the six figures.

So, about a year after starting the company, I began to revalue myself and the BrEpic brand.

The first check I ever received that had "BrEpic" written on it was for $500. I can't tell you how happy I was to deposit that check at the time, but it's funny to think now about how little that check was actually worth. And let's just say the business that paid that check – again, I'm very thankful they were an original client – was not the right fit for my mindset or company's plan to work with visionaries.

The original BrEpic rates mostly attracted non-visionaries. When I shifted to the right price point that was more in line with the true value of what BrEpic offers, I became undesirable to nickel and dimers and eventually far more alluring to big-thinking visionaries.

With BrEpic's rates now, there is zero chance that nickel and dime clients would have worked with me, and that's just fine. **BrEpic's rates and value proposition for clients only attract big-thinkers now.** I am so direct when engaging with potential new clients that it eliminates all nonsense and only reels in the cream-of-the-crop businesses and brands – true visionaries who are going for it. People who think big understand the value of investing in their businesses and will *pay more* when they know they're working with someone who's the real deal and who values himself like they value themselves.

After I started raising my rates exponentially, there at first was a sharp decline in new clients. Remember that my original clients were referring me to others in their circles – which meant more folks and businesses that did not invest heavily in their companies.

But because my rates were so much higher, I was actually making more money each month than I had previously. So I was *working less and earning more*. And I was starting to eliminate all the lower-paying clients who thought cost first and beginning to add more higher-paying clients who led with an investment-first mentality.

There were numerous times that people close to me laughed when I told them about my newer rates. They couldn't believe I had the audacity to charge that much. But they weren't the people I was targeting anyway. They weren't visionaries; they were people collecting a paycheck or others who had never taken chances growing their own businesses.

They definitely aren't laughing now.

After about three months with the new rates, a trickle of new clients began translating into more of a flood. Because BrEpic was delivering huge results to newer, higher-paying clients and they were telling their friends and business network why they were in the mainstream media all the time. So they started referring them to me.

Most of these folks don't waste much time between original discussions and actually signing contracts. They realize their business has grown by working with an elite network, and they want to add BrEpic to that mix. **Visionaries don't mind paying more – in fact, I've found that many of them would rather pay *much more* – to get results. It's all about results. That's all my clients care about. Real results.**

When I hire people now to help my business grow, I always look at their rates, and if they don't charge enough, I wonder what I'm really going to get out of it. I *want* them to charge more. This applies to the networking groups I'm a part of, website publishers, even the micro-publishers for this book. **I only work with people who value themselves and whose rates reflect that.**

I'm writing this chapter from an amazing third-story vacation rental in the Florida Keys. This morning, an incredible new client from Utah signed an amazing contract to work with my firm. Another client just RSVP'd to attend a BrEpic client-appreciation party featuring The Magic Penthouse, a super high-end magic act that's another one of my clients.

None of this would have been possible if I hadn't raised my rates. I wouldn't have been signing with these businesses. It just wouldn't have happened.

Think big. Raise your rates. People and businesses that value what you do will find you.

EPIC TAKEAWAYS:

1. Are your rates attracting the right type of clients?
2. When was the last time you raised your rates? Is it time to raise them?
3. Remember your skills are evolving and growing. Visionaries want to work with people that are evolving, growing and charging their worth.

CHAPTER TEN
VISIONARY ENTREPRENEURS ARE OFTEN THE BEST, KINDEST, MOST GIVING FOLKS OUT THERE

At his lakeside mansion that featured a giant wild prairie serving as his backyard, I interviewed one of my clients, a remarkable entrepreneur named Jack.

He had helped create a foundation where his wealth was being used to fund a program that allowed underserved students to attend colleges like Harvard and Stanford for free. He asked me if I'd rather see that money going to these students or to the government.

Seems like a pretty simple answer.

This is a grand example but almost all of the entrepreneurs I know give back in countless ways, whether it's a charity, foundation or just helping out.

In 2014, Ernst & Young interviewed more than 160 CEOs and company founders and discovered that 89 percent donated money and 70 percent donated their time to worthwhile causes. In my experience of interacting with thousands of entrepreneurs, I can think of only a few that tie into the greedy, Wall Street entrepreneur stigma. Not only is that description unfair, it's untrue!

Here's what I have learned: If you ask an entrepreneur to help you, 99.9 percent of the time, they will say yes. The whole reason this book exists is because of the advice entrepreneurs have *gladly* shared with me. They want to pay it forward because, if you are an entrepreneur and you don't ask for help or receive help from others, you have no chance of making it. In fact, Chapter 13 stresses that if someone asks you for help, *always* help them.

I'm not a hugger per se, but when I meet an entrepreneur, I usually will hug them. Entrepreneurs many times just give off a different vibe – this vibe of freedom and happy-go-lucky attitude. I told a journalist friend of mine who used to write a ton of stories on entrepreneurs and startups about this, and she said the sources for those stories always hugged her when they convened. At the time of our meeting, she wasn't covering business stories, and she said the hugging thing was one of the parts she missed about the entrepreneurial beat.

Entrepreneur magazine wrote an awesome article discussing 60 reasons why entrepreneurship is amazing. Reason No. 3, from this article, I think sums up this chapter:

"**3. You become part of a family.** *The entrepreneurial culture is almost like a big family -- and you won't find a better group of people willing to offer advice and help than fellow entrepreneurs.*"

When you surround yourself with kind, giving, simply incredible people, it's infectious. And it makes you want to give more of your time, donate more of your money and help more people!

A 2019 report from Artemis Strategy Group, an independent research firm, revealed some really interesting data.

- *On average, the median annual gift for entrepreneurs ($3,600) is 50 percent higher than non-entrepreneurs ($2,400).*
- *Two-thirds (66 percent) of entrepreneurs volunteer two or more hours a month, compared with just more than half (55 percent) of non-entrepreneurs.*
- *Six in 10 (59 percent) business owners say owning a business has influenced the way they approach their personal charitable giving—and that number rises to 68 percent for owners whose businesses generate $1 million or more in annual revenue.*
- *Millennial entrepreneurs want to be hands-on and involved. Ninety percent value charities with meaningful volunteer opportunities, and more than half say that volunteering is a chance to learn new skills relevant to their profession, compared to a third of Gen X and only 20 percent of Boomers.*
- *Effectiveness really matters to older entrepreneurs. More than 80 percent of Baby Boomer business owners prefer to give to smaller nonprofits where they know their dollars will have a big impact.*

Young, old and in-between, entrepreneurs care about helping people – especially other entrepreneurs. There is no shame in asking someone for help, especially when that person really wants to help you!

EPIC TAKEAWAYS:

1. Visionary entrepreneurs build giving back into their life and business
2. How are you "paying it forward"? Giving back? Lifting others up?
3. What are ways you can lift up and support your fellow entrepreneurs and those causes/things that are important to you?

4. Be willing to ask for help when needed. Remember, as a visionary entrepreneur you are part of a beautiful family and community of support.

LINKS:

https://www.inc.com/john-boitnott/meet-7-entrepreneurs-who-love-giving-back.html

https://www.entrepreneur.com/article/243389

https://afpglobal.org/entrepreneurs-philanthropists-how-they-give

CHAPTER ELEVEN
IF YOU'RE HAVING A BAD DAY, WEEK OR MONTH, TELL SOMEONE

Reading the first 10 chapters of this book, you might be thinking to yourself that life as an entrepreneur is all sunshine and rainbows.

It's *not*.

Being an entrepreneur and starting a business is very likely the hardest thing you will ever do. Think stress from a corporate job is unbearable? It is *nothing* compared to creating a business from ground zero.

If you can't handle ludicrously high anxiety, a roller coaster of emotions and the worst lows you can possibly imagine, you shouldn't even sniff the idea of becoming an entrepreneur.

I'm writing this chapter from a Miami Airport terminal in December 2019. A year ago at this time – despite making far more money than I ever had before, working with amazing clients and seeing my family more than any dad I know – I had never been so depressed in my life. During a family vacation, I remember riding an airboat in the Everglades, a booming noise of the air motor behind me, and feeling absolutely nothing except total helplessness.

This was a feeling *much* worse than when my salary was cut in half at DNAinfo Chicago. The only thing I can compare it to was discovering that one of my ex-girlfriends had cheated on me. Or maybe when the sweet puppy dog I had helped raise, a German Shepherd mix named Molly, chased after a rabbit and was fatally struck by a car when I was in high school. I'm telling you that I was in a far worse state of mind than when I found out that my father and brother had died.

I did my best to put on a happy face during that family vacation but knew long term that I needed serious help. This was no way to live life, in a constant state of panic, dream, sadness, loneliness and exhaustion.

So, I started to ask for help. I began seeing a therapist who focuses on anxiety and the reasons behind it – and I still try to see her once every other week. I dug deeper into myself to figure out what exactly was wrong and how I could fix it.

I started talking to a few close friends, especially those who were entrepreneurs. They had *all* been through this type of low-point before. I had a lengthy lunch with one of my mentors, Collin, who runs a thriving political consulting agency. **He said every entrepreneur he knows has been depressed at one time or another. He stressed that I had to *learn* from how I felt during this experience to know how to react positively the next time it happened.** I leaned on my wife more than I ever had before, and that's saying something.

Talking openly about my feelings helped infinitely. I was no longer alone.

I started Googling terms like "entrepreneur burnout," "entrepreneur depression" and "entrepreneur anxiety" and discovered a wealth of informative, reputable articles.

Inc published a report titled "The Psychological Price of Entrepreneurship" that revealed entrepreneurs are two times more likely to suffer from depression than non-entrepreneurs. Reasons for that included: Naturally being prone to high levels of anxiety; Difficulty not feeling in control; Large numbers of investor rejections; Stress and long working hours leading to burnout; Being sabotaged by partners, staff or investors; and struggles gaining and maintaining traction.

The report further noted that entrepreneurs are six times more likely to have ADHD, three times more likely to struggle with addiction and 11 times more likely to receive a bipolar diagnosis.

These are horrifying statistics, especially for those who aren't prepared to hear them.

Mission.org detailed the findings of a survey conducted by Dr. Michael Freeman, a clinical professor and entrepreneur who interviewed 242 entrepreneurs. Of the 242 interviewed, 49 percent reported having a mental-health condition. Depression (30 percent), ADHD (29 percent) and anxiety problems (27 percent) were the top three reported conditions, according to Freeman's interviewing.

My main issue stemmed from the anxiety of waiting for potential clients to sign contracts and whether or not current clients would renew. Instead of focusing on the positives of each month, I was dreading the thought of having no income slotted for two or three months down the road. It was paralyzing, crippling and overwhelming.

I still didn't understand how the business cycle worked – that current and potential clients work on their schedules, not mine – and they make decisions when they're ready to. **I had put so much of my self-worth into the success of BrEpic,**

that I had forgotten what was really important: My family, friends, and overall health and wellbeing.

I promised my therapist when I started seeing her, that I would put 100 percent effort into changing my mindset and working on my mental acumen. And that's what it took, over months and months and months, to start seeing major gains. It was really, really, really hard work.

It feels cathartic to share these feelings with you, and how I've changed for the better since that December 2018 airboat ride. My family took another vacation to the Everglades in December 2019 and hopped on another airboat. This time, as I sat with my oldest son in the front seat as we got covered in mucky water, I was all smiles and filled with love for my family. **Business was great, but that was not important. My mental health was strong, I had overcome depression, and I knew I would be able to handle it if it came around again.**

For current entrepreneurs, I hope you take this chapter and my story extremely seriously and please talk to someone if you need help.

For soon-to-be entrepreneurs, I'm not writing this to scare you, but to make you understand that this life can put you in *very* dark places, and you need to be prepared to challenge yourself like you never thought possible. And be willing to build in support on your journey and ask for help when/where you need it. You can and will come through if you're willing to persevere.

EPIC TAKEAWAYS:

1. The journey of an entrepreneur is not all sunshine and rainbows
2. Entrepreneurship is a personally challenging and powerful journey
3. Be willing to ask for and receive help
4. Be clear on your priorities
5. Learn what matters most to you and how to move you and your business forward
6. Entrepreneurs have the opportunity to personally and professionally grow

LINKS:

https://www.inc.com/magazine/201309/jessica-bruder/psychological-price-of-entrepreneurship.html

https://medium.com/the-mission/12-quotes-on-entrepreneur-burnout-and-depression-from-those-whove-walked-the-path-a0d62a3ed389

CHAPTER TWELVE

YOU NEVER KNOW WHERE YOUR NEXT CLIENT WILL COME FROM. TREAT EVERY MEETING, PHONE CALL AND OPPORTUNITY AS IMPORTANT

Allstate was BrEpic's first major client. I signed with them just a few months after people found out I was running an actual business.

You might be wondering how a Fortune 500 company wanted to work with a one-man, just-opened PR shop that was trying to figure out its business model, and you'd be right to wonder!

Here's what happened. One day, while I was working on drumming up business, I received a random email from an executive at Allstate asking if I could be a judge in one of their contests featuring inspirational teens across the country. Somehow, Allstate had found me because I had written inspirational stories about awesome teens at DNAinfo Chicago and other journalism stops, and I had a pretty large social media following. At the time, I had about 20,000 followers. Laura, the person at Allstate who contacted me, *didn't even know I had a company.* She thought I was still a journalist!

I looked at the date of the event, and it conflicted with one of my client meetings, so I emailed back to Laura that I couldn't make it, but I'd be happy to meet with her in person to discuss future judging opportunities.

A few weeks later, we had a great lunch in Downtown Northbrook. I told her I wasn't a journalist anymore, but that I had this cool, just-announced PR firm that was getting great results for its clients with a unique model of writing and pitching stories. And Laura said that's exactly what Allstate's major nonprofit – The Allstate Foundation – was looking for to tell stories about incredible teens and young adults across the country.

Flash forward about one month, and I was taking a photo with Laura at Allstate's Northbrook headquarters to announce that Allstate was BrEpic's newest client!

Here's the lesson learned from the Allstate example: Take every meeting, phone call, email and other opportunity seriously. You simply don't know if it will be a dead end or lead to one of your greatest business opportunities.

I have a good memory, but I've met so many people that sometimes I can't place a name. That happened in early 2019 when an advertising executive named Scot at one of my former newspaper employers reached out and said one of his clients needed PR help. I had doubts as I didn't remember this person and the company he mentioned did not sound interesting on paper. He told me the company would be reaching out soon.

"Soon" turned into two months, and I had forgotten about the initial conversation. So when the company's marketing director mentioned that Scot gave them my contact information, I had no idea what she was talking about.

But I took the phone call seriously and heard more about the company, which was experiencing huge growth and was implementing some state-of-the-art, groundbreaking technology that would really help people. Turns out, this healthcare business was led by a visionary who wanted its story told to the masses, and they heard that BrEpic could do just that.

A week later, I had another great client!

The randomness of running a business can provide truly beyond-belief highs, especially when an out-of-the-blue conversation leads to a huge contract.

No matter how crazy it seems, stories like this happen all the time with businesses. If you treat interactions seriously and follow up, it can generate tremendous wealth and opportunities.

EPIC TAKEAWAYS:

1. Treat Every call, meeting, and contact seriously
2. Be open to where a conversation and call could go
3. Do your follow up!

CHAPTER THIRTEEN

IF SOMEONE ASKS FOR HELP, ALWAYS HELP THEM

I am surrounded by entrepreneurs who gladly give up their time to help others who ask.

It's infectious.

When I was a journalist, I'd always try to mentor cub reporters, students or recent graduates to try to help them find jobs, develop story ideas or just meet to answer questions.

As a business owner, the requests for assistance have increased tenfold, and I'm more than happy to pay it forward. **At least 2-3 times a week, someone asks to speak on the phone or meet to hear about how I built BrEpic, or to get out of journalism and into PR, or to tell me about their relative or friend who is looking for a job.**

I will *always* help them.

Let it be clear that I'm not writing this chapter for any praise, but to make it known that when someone asks you for help, you should do your best to help them. This is not about others returning the favor. **This is about doing the right thing.**

I especially like helping people find jobs. As I know all too well from having gone through it, landing a full-time job is a nightmare. It's a horrible, mind-draining process. A black hole inside a black hole.

I spend at least an hour a week trying to help people find jobs. Sometimes they offer to pay. I would never take their money for that.

I use my LinkedIn page as a platform to help others find jobs. With more than 17,000 followers, my LinkedIn is a great place for others to use as a job service. I routinely tag and highlight people without jobs on LinkedIn to help get the ball rolling for them. Many times, it leads to great intros and even positions. The ultimate example of this is when I recommended a person for a full-time job at one of my clients, and that person essentially replaced my vendor role with the client. So that effort *literally took money out of my pocket*, which is just fine by me.

I've helped others launch their own PR firms. I've helped other PR firms find talented reporters, social media experts, and other employees and freelancers. Like others have inspired me to think big, I encourage countless folks to emerge from nickel-and-dime mentalities and dream like a visionary.

During every meeting, I ask people how can I help them or what types of intros would be beneficial. There's no use having an amazing network of visionaries if you can't introduce them to each other.

Huffington Post in 2017 scribed a great piece titled "10 facts that prove helping others is a key to achieving happiness." One of the facts, according to a study from the National Institutes of Health, noted that helping others improves friendships and can build lasting bonds. Another, according to United Health Group, said helping someone can make you feel like you can take on the world. The UHG said helping also lowers stress and enriches people's sense of purpose.

Again, the mojo of being around positive-thinking entrepreneurs rubs off on me every single day. And science tells us why. According to a 2010 study by researchers at UCLA, and University of Cambridge and University of Plymouth in the United Kingdom, kindness is simply contagious. **"When we see someone else help another person it gives us a good feeling, which in turn causes us to go out and do something altruistic ourselves," the study said.**

Another one of my mentors is a financial entrepreneurial genius named Gary who was first in his graduating class of U.S. Army Rangers. During a lunch where we both dined on shrimp salad, Gary talked about how the validity of helping others dates back to Plato's thinking and teaching edicts. Plato's goal in life was to help others reach a state of fulfillment and happiness. Plato also said that helping others benefits them but also makes the helper feel useful and satisfied.

Before he died, my father's last living brother, Stan, told me to read Plato's *The Republic* when I was a college student in the late 1990s. I didn't really understand the book's logic when I read it then, but it all started to make sense when Gary was talking about Plato at that lunch.

The whole point of this book is to share the knowledge I've gained to help you in your lives, businesses and careers. **Helping people will benefit you in endless ways, make you a much better person and lead to others paying it forward as well. Everyone wins!**

EPIC TAKEAWAYS:

1. Be willing to help others
2. Helping feels good and lowers stress
3. When others ask for help, be willing to share openly
4. Be willing to introduce others to connection that will help them
5. When we all lean in and help one another we ALL WIN!

LINKS:

https://www.huffpost.com/entry/
international-day-of-happiness-helping-_n_6905446

https://helix.northwestern.edu/article/
kindness-contagious-new-study-finds

https://exploringyourmind.com/
best-plato-said-understanding-world/

CHAPTER FOURTEEN

FIND AT LEAST 2-3 GOOD MENTORS AND LISTEN TO THEM

The global financial services company Kabbage interviewed 200 small business owners across the U.S. and discovered that only 22 percent had mentors when they started the business.

The study also revealed that 92 *percent* of those small business owners agreed that mentors had a direct impact on growth and the *very survival* of their business.

I have been blessed to have several terrific mentors from the very start of this crazy journey. I would have been completely lost and rudderless without their guidance.

The first was my best friend Chris – again, he's now a client. He and I had daily conversations about entrepreneurial life and what I could expect. Even though I was never truly prepared for the ups and downs until I actually experienced them, at least I had some background about what could happen. The success of his first company was instrumental in giving me the belief that I could do the same with mine.

Another great mentor has been Laura, a PR executive at a giant firm. She was a former journalist, had her own thriving firm and then was hired by the larger firm and became their employee. She was key in giving me advice to raise my rates and only deal with cream-of-the-crop clients. **Her passion for her career also fueled the passion for mine. She was living a great life as well – *and putting her family first.***

Collin, the visionary political strategist, is one of my favorite mentors. He's much younger than me but he has much, much, much more entrepreneurial wisdom to share. He built his company from nothing more than 10 years ago, starting with local school board elections to now running some of the most important campaigns in the Midwest. He mentors countless people, all while taking time to swim with great white sharks and climb at the Grand Canyon. He is exactly the type of person that I want to be, and he is always challenging me to constantly be better, do more and grow BrEpic.

I didn't have a true visionary mentality until conversations with Collin started. When we first met, he said I had to start hiring people, and if I didn't the company would never grow. That was about two years ago, and I finally started implementing his advice in 2019 (Chapter 24). **During a recent meeting, he said that two years into the future, I will barely be working *in* the business, but almost exclusively *on* the business. Now I have the mindset to not only understand what he's saying, but to execute his plans for my business as well.**

In the previous chapter, I briefly mentioned another mentor, Gary. The first time I talked with Gary, I knew that was he truly different – in a genius type of way. There are very few entrepreneurs like him, even at the highest level. His brain is moving so fast, that it's sometimes hard to keep up with him, but I knew that I had to seek his guidance on a quarterly basis. Gary leads a wildly successful financial company, creates wealth and value for some of the top folks in society, and takes a ton of time off where he's completely off the grid. **He also insisted that I join Strategic Coach, the entrepreneurial group that has completely changed my life as you'll discover in the next chapter.**

Having these amazing people as mentors has built the fabric of BrEpic and skyrocketed me toward an even more amazing future. *Every entrepreneur – every person really – should have at least two great mentors in their lives.*

Forbes in 2018 published an article titled "Three reasons you need a mentor" that is a must-read for any business owner. **The three reasons were: Good mentors help you set a measurable goal; good mentors never let you settle and become complacent; and good mentors will share personal experiences that inspire and motivate you.**

This is exactly what my mentors have done for me! Without direction, it's extremely difficult to succeed in business or in life. Consistently being challenged keeps me humble, excited and passionate for BrEpic and for what's next. And learning from my mentors' experiences has prepared me for potential roadblocks on my business highway. Plus, it's allowed me to become a mentor for numerous others.

There's another great column from Inc that reveals "10 reasons why a mentor is a must." The reasons are similar to the Forbes article, but the last line of the Inc story is my favorite.

"Having a mentor is not a sign of weakness; it shows you are smart enough and are driven enough to succeed."

Please, please, please do not be in that 78 percent of small business owners who don't have a mentor when you launch your business. This road is hard enough. You need great folks to help you find your pathway to entrepreneurial greatness.

EPIC TAKEAWAYS:

1. Find a mentor that you admire and want to learn from
2. Listen to what your mentor(s) advise and implement their ideas/suggestions
3. Set measurable goals and grow
4. Remember you don't have to do it all on your own

LINKS:

https://www.kabbage.com/greenhouse/article/data-shows-mentors-are-vital-to-small-business-success/

https://www.forbes.com/sites/forbesbusinessdevelopmentcouncil/2018/01/09/three-reasons-you-need-a-mentor/#3640f7ea1eeb

https://www.inc.com/john-rampton/10-reasons-why-a-mentor-is-a-must.html

JOIN GREAT NETWORKING GROUPS WITH HIGH-LEVEL PEOPLE. (STRATEGIC COACH AND PROVISORS ARE MY TWO FAVORITES)

When I was a journalist, I had a giant network, but I didn't know *how to network*.

Networking is a science where the most important ingredient is interacting with the right type of people. If you talk to 1,000 people and all 1,000 are nickel and dimers, it's a total waste of time.

For more than a year, I struggled greatly to find my tribe of the right groups. I tried chambers of commerce – I recommend not doing this ever – and other small-scale operations that were filled with folks without vision, deep pockets or interesting businesses. I was desperate to get away from these groups but couldn't locate an alternative.

I started asking some of my high-level friends where they belong or where they'd like to belong. Kristin – the attorney who told me that running a business takes two full years to figure out – recommended I look into an organization called <u>ProVisors</u>. It was vetted, featured prominent lawyers, financial planners, marketers and other CEOs, and it had a decent-sized annual entry fee.

I applied and after a month or two was accepted into the group, which has locations in Chicago, Southern California, Boston and a few other big cities around the country. In Chicago, there are more than a dozen groups; I attend mine monthly and get to guest at others. After meetings, members are paired up and schedule lunches or coffee meetings. You actually get to *know* people.

Immediately, I could tell the people in ProVisors were different. Much different. They were successful, a few were visionaries, they were super nice, and they were going places.

Soon, I started becoming good friends with many of the folks in my group and others throughout the network. Within a few months, I signed my first client from ProVisors. That led to several more. **Remember: Your clients become your friends, and your friends become your clients.**

In the year-plus I've been in ProVisors, I've 30x'd my investment and met countless awesome people. I probably receive a good referral from a ProVisors member once every three weeks. My directness appeals to these people. I routinely tell those in my network about ProVisors as well; the organization awarded me a funny trophy that said "ProVisors King of Candidate Referrals" because I make so many intros for potential new members.

And because ProVisors is national, I envision business opportunities expanding to endless parts of the country.

If ProVisors was the foundation for great networking opportunities, Strategic Coach slingshot my business and mindset to limits I never thought possible – and very quickly. Strategic Coach was founded more than 30 years ago and has without a doubt been the biggest game-changer my business and I have experienced.

Oh my God, Strategic Coach is incredible!!!!

It's heavily vetted and is only for entrepreneurs on an international level. Participants' businesses have to make at least $200,000 annually to join, and yearly dues are five figures. Before I started a business, I never would have thought of spending $10,000-plus on anything other than a house, car or engagement ring.

Things have changed.

I joined Strategic Coach in early 2019 because most of my really, really successful networking friends told me to join. They said I *had* to. Because it's all entrepreneurs and the yearly investment weeds out all the nonsense, it only attracts visionaries – people that think big.

My group meets quarterly in Chicago, but I am the only person whose business is based in Illinois. Everyone else flies in. The entrepreneurs in this program are out of this world. They all think like me. They all can afford BrEpic's services. They understand the value of investing in their businesses. They are all in growth mode – to a 10x level.

Because of Strategic Coach, I've learned how to scale BrEpic, take more "Free Days" – or days where you literally do zero work for all 24 hours – supercharge my network, and think of myself more like an entertainer in terms of getting paid. Entertainers receive big payments when they "perform," much like when entrepreneurs perform their Unique Ability. In my case, it's writing stories for clients and pitching them to media. Then, like entertainers, entrepreneurs likely will take significant time off before they are paid again. This way of thinking has alleviated all the stress I had before when I wanted to receive every two weeks like I had when I was a journalist. It was life-changing.

In addition to the quarterly meetings, there are two checkup meetings with an individual coach each quarter. My coach, Amy, is the best! Because I'm local, I drive to see her for lunch instead of calling her. She has kept me on track and given me endless ideas to propel BrEpic to unprecedented levels. And it all starts with creating more free time while partnering with better and better clients. I am so thankful for her guidance.

I invest a significant amount of time and resources into these two groups, and it's only the beginning. I recently joined Entrepreneurs' Organization's Accelerator Program in Chicago for businesses with revenues of between $250,000 and $1 million. The goal of the Accelerator, which is a $5,000 yearly investment, is to boost companies over the $1 million mark and intro the main EO program. I can't wait to start!

As I've doubled down on BrEpic's core business strategy and process, I will continue to double down on high-level networking groups that put me in a room with the right people who are just like me.

EPIC TAKEAWAYS:

1. Join great networking groups
2. Look for groups of "your" people
3. Be willing to invest in the groups you join and fully participate
4. Build time off into your schedule
5. Treat yourself as the "Talent" you are

LINKS:

https://www.provisors.com/

https://www.strategiccoach.com/

BE PATIENT. THINGS TAKE TIME. THE BUSINESS CYCLE CAN BE SLOW, ESPECIALLY WITH LARGER COMPANIES

As a journalist, the only main term that really matters is *deadline.*

Deadline. Deadline. Deadline. Deadline. Deadline. Must file before the deadline. Get ... it ... done!!!

As a journalist, you are constantly under pressure to meet deadlines every single day, and then do it all over again and again and again and again, year after year after year. It is a hectic pace that is not for everyone and burns many folks out in a few years.

As a journalist for more than two decades, I was faced with this daily deadline pressure – either as a reporter or editor – and this madness just became part of my fabric. It's in your blood and your life cycle blends with the chaos.

Life as a business owner is, for the most part, the complete opposite. Things on this end can move at a snail's pace. It has been my biggest challenge to go from 0-60 in 3 seconds to 0-60 in 3 months.

Now terms that are part of my life include *compliance*, *procurement* and, most importantly, *patience*. I have zero patience; even when I was a reporter, super-fast editors asked me to slow down. I can write a chapter of this book in about 10-15 minutes. When clients ask how long it will take me to send them the first draft of the story, I usually tell them it will arrive later that day, and they look at me like I'm some kind of mad scientist.

But most people aren't like that, especially in the business world. **They make decisions slowly. From what I've learned, the *larger* the company, the *longer* it takes for anything to get done – from an initial meeting to get scheduled, to an actual contract being signed.**

As a journalist, sources usually bend backwards to accommodate your schedule. As a business owner, the role is flipped – your schedule routinely revolves around clients' or potential clients' work weeks.

A large university client initially reached out to me in October 2017. They were very interested to earn more exposure for their remarkable students, faculty and alumni, and many of them were involved with ground-breaking companies and research. We discussed a potential contract, and, five minutes after we hung up the phone, I sent them the proposal.

The contract wasn't signed until May of 2018 – almost three-quarters of a year later. In between were months of waiting patiently – for me it was excruciatingly painful – to see how the contract weaved its way through procurement and compliance offices, making sure every I was dotted, every T was crossed. My brain doesn't work like that, but for big university systems, I can see why they are so thorough.

Organically and probably because of my lack of patience, my business has gravitated toward working with businesses in rapid, early growth that make decisions quickly and

effectively. The CEOs and founders of those organizations think like I do: As in, let's just get this done and start earning huge results!

But I like working with really large clients, too, because they have endless story ideas in media markets across the world. It doesn't hurt that they have deep pockets, too.

So, I've had to adapt – slowly but surely – to their way of thinking and their process of slogging through the details and minutiae. And when those bigger clients tell me, "hey it might be six months or a year before we get back to you," *they actually mean it.* And I now understand that when they say they'll get back to me in half a year, I believe them.

About a year into BrEpic's existence, a national banking institution called me to help run a national campaign about how it was helping underserved communities across the country with various major loans and programs. Numerous meetings followed in the subsequent six months, and they were about to sign an amazing, long-term contract with BrEpic. But then they merged with another bank, and it put the kibosh on all deals with outside vendors.

About a year later, the contact I had been talking to from the bank's national office put me in touch with a more Midwestern contact who was interested in partnering with BrEpic. As of this book's publication, discussions are still taking place, but I now have a much greater maturity in dealing with the big boys of business and playing the waiting game more effectively.

I wouldn't be surprised if a deal down the road with this company – even if it takes 5-10 years – is much bigger than the original one I was offered.

That's just how it works.

EPIC TAKEAWAYS:

1. Be patient with the decision-making cycle and process.
2. Remember, the larger the company frequently the longer the decision-making process...but the more consistent/on-going projects that can be available.
3. In your business planning and business model, allow time for both shorter and longer decision-making cycles. (Hot tip: If you don't know your current sales cycle, make sure to start tracking it from first sales conversation to contract signed and first payment in your accounts.)

CHAPTER SEVENTEEN

GIVE BACK, START A SCHOLARSHIP FUND, HELP THE COMMUNITY, AND DO SOMETHING TO PAY IT FORWARD

By the time this book publishes, the first "BrEpic Award" will have been given to one of my clients, an awesome private high school called The Chicago Academy for the Arts.

I'm donating a yearly amount to the school to help students who are entrepreneurially inclined. The Academy is chock-full of genius-level art students – either in dance, painting, acting or other disciplines – but there are others who have already started their own nonprofits and companies. The BrEpic award will assist those types of students who are already dreaming big.

And this is only the beginning. As BrEpic grows, I plan to donate more and more and more to my clients, charities and other worthwhile causes.

I don't have to do this. I *want* to do this.

What's the point of having success if you can't pay it forward and help someone else? That's never made any sense to me.

Chapter 10 discussed and provided data how entrepreneurs are more giving than non-entrepreneurs. And there is everything to *gain* by giving.

Carrie Morgridge, VP of The Morgridge Family Foundation – a group that makes investments to transform communities through education, the arts and other avenues – wrote a great piece in Success magazine that noted: **"Whoever you are, no matter how much or how little you have, your gift matters. The smallest, seemingly unimportant, donation can transform a life. And the best news is that giving transforms two lives: the one who receives and the one who gives."**

I have gained so much joy from starting this award with The Chicago Academy for the Arts. I can't wait to see what amazing student receives the honor and donation!

BrEpic in its first year also honored The Allstate Foundation with its annual BrEpic Founders' Award – given to a client that has been a great partner and had tremendous success in terms of mainstream media appearances. As part of the award, BrEpic made a donation to one of The Allstate Foundation's partners, the nonprofit We Are Able – which works to raise awareness about the importance of creating a society where everyone has an equal opportunity to succeed and become leaders within their community, as well as educate people about proper disability etiquette.

I'm also a Chicago Innovation Mentor at Matter, an incredible incubator for healthcare startups, volunteer bell ringer for The Salvation Army and a longtime Journalism Chair for the University of Illinois College of Media Alumni Board.

I've found that, for the most part, the more successful the entrepreneur, the more she or he gives back.

As BrEpic grows, so will its donations to great causes, and my time to help others live their own dreams.

Giving back is what's *really* exciting about building a business.

EPIC TAKEAWAYS:

1. Look for ways to give back
2. Build giving back in your business in a way that is meaningful to you
3. Be creative about finding ways to give back...have fun with it
4. The more you grow, the more you can give, and the more joy you will have in helping others

LINKS:

https://www.success.com/what-do-you-get-from-giving-3-things-actually/

https://www.weable.org/the-campaign/

CHAPTER EIGHTEEN

IT'S OK TO DO CRAZY THINGS LIKE JUMPING OUT OF AN AIRPLANE

Time and time again as BrEpic grew and grew, I asked my fellow entrepreneurs how it felt to run a business.

And time and time again, they said that it felt like jumping out an airplane and not knowing whether the parachute would open.

To celebrate BrEpic's two-year anniversary and its success, I decided to see how it felt to jump out an *actual airplane* and compare it to the ups and downs of building BrEpic.

Keep in mind, I am *terrified* of heights – or at least I used to be. During my early days as a journalist in Michigan City, I hosted a small TV show called "Behind The Scenes With Justin Breen" where I ventured around the community and did fun things like charter fishing for salmon in Lake Michigan and indoor rock climbing. One of the episodes had planned for me to go skydiving, and the thought of that kept me awake at night for weeks. Thank God that that episode got canceled.

But as an entrepreneur, my fear factor has plummeted. **I have *conquered* fear because of BrEpic's success. If you can build a business, I'm convinced you can pretty much do anything.**

So, in August 2019, I booked a skydiving excursion at Skydive Midwest, just over the border in Wisconsin. I went up on a Monday, and, because of cloudy conditions, the dive was canceled.

Now in the past, I would have been really excited that the dive didn't happen, but I was more annoyed now because I really wanted to do it.

So, I canceled some of my meetings on Tuesday and drove to the tiny airport again. This time, the weather was perfect, and the guides essentially told me I had nothing to worry about. And, honestly, I was totally calm...well, most of the time.

I was strapped to an expert skydiver named Keith, who had made hundreds of jumps. He had awesome dreadlocks and said he was thrilled to jump with me and said I should just enjoy the experience. We walked onto a small plane that had a clear plastic door that slid up and down to allow divers to jump.

And then we took off and climbed higher and higher and higher – 15,000 feet up – into the air.

There were about 4 skydivers strapped to their guides on our journey, and I volunteered to jump first. The most scared I got was when they opened the plastic door and we were at the apex of our flight, and looking down almost three miles is a pretty gnarly feeling.

Then we jumped.

The next 60-or-so seconds were among the most remarkable in my life. It's a hard feeling to describe unless you've actually done it. You're dropping so fast and the wind is so powerful – and it's *bitterly cold* that high in the sky – it's just crazy. I had a videographer dive with us as well, and he took awesome footage of the jump. The videographer,

Austin, also reached out and let me grab his hands as we spun around in a free fall. **It was epic. Truly.**

After 60 seconds, the parachute did open – I had no doubts it would – and Keith and I floated through a cloud and eventually to the ground.

It indeed was a similar feeling to running a business – chaos, total exhilaration, some relief and immense joy of accomplishing something really, really big that most people would never even think about, let alone do.

The reward was worth the risk.

As an entrepreneur, **I've learned not only is it OK to take risks, but that it's encouraged to take the right risks. The most successful entrepreneurs I know make calculated risks – betting on themselves and their businesses – and learning along the way.** These visionaries are the ones who become my clients. Very few of the safety-net entrepreneurs in my network become my clients because they don't have a big vision; they're comfortable being so-so, above average, risk-averse. And that's fine, but it doesn't mold with my way of thinking.

WebMD published a great report about risk-takers finding more happiness in their lives. German researchers interviewed more than 20,000 people about their risky behavior and found "people who enjoyed taking risks were more content with their lives."

This shouldn't surprise you in any way. I can't tell you how many people I've talked to who are in their 50s, 60s and 70s who say "I wish I would have done that when I was younger" or "my business could have been much bigger if I had only had bigger dreams" or something to that effect. It's a lingering, regretful feeling that is just simply sad.

The visionary folks I work with leave nothing on the table. *They don't have regrets.* Many of them have also done crazy things like jumping out an airplane. And when I tell them I did it, too, you can see them smiling ear to ear.

EPIC TAKEAWAYS:

1. Be willing to take calculated risks
2. Be willing to be on yourself and your business
3. Leave nothing on the table
4. Build your business with no regrets
5. The reward is worth the risk

LINK:

https://www.webmd.com/balance/news/20050919/are-risk-takers-happier

CHAPTER NINETEEN

BE A GREAT EXAMPLE FOR YOUR CHILDREN. SHOW THEM THE AMAZING LIFE THEY CAN HAVE BY BEING AN ENTREPRENEUR AND WHAT HARD WORK CAN LEAD TO

One or two times a week, I take my kids to Dunkin' Donuts for breakfast.

My wife works set hours, so after I run in the very early morning (Chapter 25), I'm with the kids for a few hours before dropping them off at school.

So, we go out to breakfast a lot to have "man's time" and talk about the day before and the upcoming school activities for the day.

At one of these breakfasts – we always split a few toasted bagels or some donuts – I saw a dad with who I'm assuming were his three young daughters. He was nicely dressed in a shirt and tie, and super happy to be there. I could tell he was having a great time.

There were some cars in the parking lot, but one stood out – a fully decked-out, just-washed white pickup truck with a landscaping company name on it. I saw the truck and guaranteed to my kids that when this nicely dressed man and the girls went to the parking lot, they would go into the truck because the man was an entrepreneur and the landscaping company was his.

Sure enough, the man and the girls left the restaurant and hopped into the truck; FYI when the kids weren't watching, I asked the man if he owned the company, and he said yes.

After the owner and the girls departed, **I told my kids that he had the freedom to do what he wanted – and when he wanted – and drive that awesome pickup truck because he was the owner of a company.**

I reinforced the idea that the man's feeling of satisfaction – both in work and personal life – many times is the result of entrepreneurial vision and implementation. And I note that that's how I feel every single day because of the entrepreneurial freedom I enjoy on a daily basis.

I tell my sons I can spend all this quality time with them because I'm an entrepreneur. That freedom allows me to set my own schedule and see them when I want to. I stress that most dads don't get this truly great opportunity to spend this much time with their children.

I've been installing this mindset in Jake and Chase since they were 5 and 3 years old, respectively. Chase has been helping me file receipts and other tax items in BrEpic file cabinets since he was in diapers. He tells me all the time he wants to take over BrEpic even though he doesn't know what BrEpic does.

A few days after the Robert Feder article revealed I had launched my own firm, I received a call from the president of one of Chicago's largest PR firms. He asked me bluntly what I wanted from my business and noted that his firm was always looking for talented people like me.

Without hesitation, I told him that I was hoping that BrEpic would become a worldwide brand working with amazing businesses and brands, and, more importantly, that my sons would eventually take over. He said he was pleased with that response.

One of the best parts about BrEpic is showing my sons what hard work, a giant network filled with great people and executing some neat ideas can lead to. Almost every day, **I tell them that regardless of what they do in life, they need to work with the best people – the ones that are truly visionary and believe in helping others.** I don't care what my children's majors are in college, but I told them the one deal breaker is they must take business classes and especially something that focuses on entrepreneurism. I learned absolutely nothing about business – or how the world really works – in college, and I'm not going to let my sons be as ill-prepared as I was.

Entrepreneur posted a terrific article titled "5 Benefits of Teaching Young Children About Entrepreneurship" that I consider a must-read. **The story noted that kids who are taught business early develop a better work ethic, a stronger appreciation for money, creative thinking, improved people skills and better goal setting.** I've found that my kids have started to develop all of these traits, **while also learning how to accept failure** – and learn from failure.

Where I live, I've noticed endless amounts of helicopter parents that enable their children and don't allow them to fail. Everybody wins nonsense. I have personally seen how that type of parenting can destroy families and people because when folks actually do fail, they can't handle it – and never recover from it.

Learning how to fail from being an entrepreneur has made me *encourage* my kids to fail. **It's *ok* to fail. I tell them that all** the entrepreneurs I know have failed miserably and have never given up. That's what's made them great.

Sara Blakely, the founder of Spanx, told Entrepreneur that her father asked her every week what she and her siblings failed at. "If we didn't have something, he would be disappointed," Blakely said. **"It changed my mindset at an early age that failure is not the outcome, failure is not trying. Don't be afraid to fail."**

I love it when people say to me, "wow your kids are really tough and bold." Their teachers say all the time that my children are very independent. And I tell them that's because they're probably future entrepreneurs like their dad.

EPIC TAKEAWAYS:

1. You can build the life you want as an entrepreneur
2. Set your schedule and priorities clearly
3. Embrace the freedom and joy of owning your own business
4. Part of being a successful entrepreneur is being willing to fail and learn and grow from your failures.
5. Failure is a step on the journey, not the end of it...be resilient and learn and grow from failures
6. Failures can help you build something great
7. Be proud of being an entrepreneur and share the gift of it with future generations

LINKS:

https://www.entrepreneur.com/article/292631

https://www.entrepreneur.com/article/219367

THINK ABOUT THE PEOPLE WHO HAVE IMPACTED YOU AND THANK THEM BEFORE IT'S TOO LATE

There isn't a day that goes by where I don't think about my dad and have regrets that I didn't have a proper goodbye with him.

The memories of the last time I saw him lying helplessly on that emergency room hospital bed still haunt me.

I would pretty much do anything to see him one more time just to say thank you for being a great dad.

Unfortunately, that's not possible.

As a journalist, I made the same mistake with one of my mentors, Bill Nangle, the late executive editor at The Times of Northwest Indiana. He was grooming me to take over for him in his final years, and we spent hours in his car driving to meetings to and from Indianapolis. During those rides, we talked about life and the importance of family. I had been married at that point, but I didn't have children yet.

The last time I saw him was at a dinner at a Downtown Chicago high-end steakhouse where he and I dined with our wives. I had just taken the job at DNAinfo Chicago, and he wanted to have dinner before I departed The Times. We had a great meal, but at the end, I somehow forgot to tell him how much his guidance had meant to me. He died about a year later. I still feel badly about it.

Huffington Post published an article titled "**The Benefits Of Gratitude: Why Saying Thank You Matters**" that stressed **these two simple words we learned as children "have a profound impact on our daily outlook, our ability to chart a course of success and most importantly to be happy."** NBC News highlighted a study from the University of California San Diego's School of Medicine that said "the practice of gratitude can have dramatic and lasting effects in a person's life and it can lower blood pressure, improve immune function and facilitate more efficient sleep." The study also "found that people who were more grateful actually had better heart health, specifically less inflammation and healthier heart rhythms."

Since starting BrEpic, I changed my "thank you tune" tremendously. It feels great to constantly thank people – and sincerely mean it. I try to thank my mentors in writing or in person at least once a quarter. Same goes for my clients, networking colleagues, friends and everyone in between. And **once you start saying thank you, it becomes contagious.** I've found that the people I hang out with are always sending me thank you texts or emails, or acknowledging something I did for them on a social media post. Not only does it feel awesome to be the recipient of these messages, but many times it leads to potential business opportunities.

Saying thank you literally takes only a few seconds out of your day, but it can lead to a lifetime of joy. I'll never make the mistake of forgetting to thank people before it's too late again.

EPIC TAKEAWAYS:

1. Thank those who have impacted you and your life
2. Build in the practice of thanking people regularly
3. Be grateful
4. Thanking others is good for your health, business and relationships, and it feels great
5. Don't wait, start thanking people today

LINKS:

https://www.entrepreneur.com/article/219367

https://www.today.com/health/be-thankful-science-says-gratitude-good-your-health-t58256

CHAPTER TWENTY-ONE
CELEBRATE SUCCESSES AND APPRECIATE WHAT YOU'VE BUILT

Last year, I threw a huge BrEpic party with clients and friends on a Chicago River tour boat.

I rented out the whole boat and invited some truly great people. The catering was provided by Gino's East Pizza. We had a dozen-or-so deep-dish pies.

For about two hours, the boat traveled on the Chicago River and then to Lake Michigan. Most of the guests sat on the top level and just admired the skyline view.

I had organized smaller client appreciation parties before in suites at baseball games and a horse racing track, but this was *different*. This tiny little company had been successful enough to easily afford this mega-awesome event.

In the first two years of BrEpic, that night had been one of the few times I had taken a step back and thought, *wow what an amazing thing this truly is!*

As an entrepreneur, you're so busy grinding, grinding, GRINDING, that it's sometimes tough to appreciate the accomplishments of building something special from nothing.

Now, at least once a day, **I try to celebrate successes and wins** – I talked about the Win Streak app in Chapter 7 – and think about how thankful I am to have this life and this business.

I've learned that from being an entrepreneur, it's OK to be happy. It's OK to have big parties. It's OK to say no to people. It's OK to think really big.

It is not *bragging*. It is not *showy*. It is *celebrating*!

Most of my clients celebrate in a big way, too. One of my clients is a healthcare company that runs urgent care clinics. When they acquired a few competitor locations, they shut down offices later that day and set up an impromptu party at a high-end Chicago bar. The CEO was super excited when I told him I thought the same way, too.

The great speaker and coach Tony Robbins talked about this topic in a <u>blog</u> post called "How do you celebrate your success?" He listed seven key ways people show gratitude for their accomplishments, including: "I celebrate with someone I really care about. We just do whatever comes to us in that moment – no plan, we just go and experience it" and "I look for a way to share it with the people that made it possible."

An article from Entrepreneur detailed a study from Washington State University that showed "that **taking the time to savor and dwell on pleasurable experiences greatly improves the mental and physical well-being of individuals.** Most importantly, it has a measurable and positive impact on subjects' future ability to deal with stressful situations."

Inc provided more detail in a post that said **"busy entrepreneurs can burn out if they don't take time to celebrate the small stuff"** and when we focus on accomplishments, "it sparks the reward circuitry of our brains. This causes a chain reaction as the brain releases chemicals that stimulate feelings of pride, excitement, and happiness. It makes us want to dig deeper into our next achievement."

Strategic Coach talks a great deal about positive mindset in its "The Gap And The Gain" mentality. Essentially, it looks at how you think about your life, in a positive or negative way. For example: Those who look at things in the "Gap" mentality might be upset that they made $300,000 in a year instead of $400,000 – a gap of $100,000. The "Gain" mentality – where I live now – is more like "OH MY GOD I MADE $300,000 THIS YEAR!!!!!"

I've learned that people who live in the "Gap" never seem to be happy or satisfied with their lives or businesses. But the ones who are in the "Gain" appear to appreciate everything, every single win, all their accomplishments. And that mindset absolutely attracts others who feel the same way.

For the launch of this book, I'm planning the biggest BrEpic event yet. It really is going to be epic, an absolutely epic celebration! Because that's what life is all about – and how it should be!

EPIC TAKEAWAYS:

1. Celebrate your successes and wins
2. Celebrating improves our mental and physical wellness
3. Celebrating encourages more successes
4. Remember to focus on the "gains" and not the "gaps"
5. Having a gain focus is attractive to more gain focused individuals, prospects and clients
6. Celebrate today...don't wait

LINKS:

https://www.tonyrobbins.com/mind-meaning/
how-do-you-celebrate-your-success/

https://www.entrepreneur.com/article/273942

https://www.inc.com/marla-tabaka/no-time-to-slow-
down-celebrate-your-small-wins-what-if-i-told-you-it-
could-make-you-more-productive.html

https://now.strategiccoach.com/
the-gap-and-the-gain-ebook

CHAPTER TWENTY-TWO

LEARN FROM TOUGH TIMES, BAD CLIENTS OR DEALS THAT HAVE GONE UNDER AT THE LAST MINUTE. IT'S JUST PART OF BUSINESS

I can't tell you how many times a potential client has told me they would sign a contract and then I never heard from them again.

There have been numerous other occasions when a potential client did sign the contract and then decided to back out at the last minute without explanation.

People are people, and some people just happen to be flat-out liars or disingenuous. Some have great intentions but struggle with commitment and follow through. I've learned that when many people sound too good to be true, they are usually in fact too good to be true.

My rates and directness have weeded out almost all of that garbage. I found that people who talk a lot about what they'd like to do but haven't executed or accomplished any of it are silenced pretty quickly when I tell them about my process and what an investment with BrEpic looks like. **The people who are direct like me and are real business people just**

get it. They *say less and do more*. Visionaries don't make excuses; they just get things done.

I worked for months in therapy to accomplish what seems like a simple task now. When people backed out of deals or lied to me or delayed things, I internalized it and put tremendous pressure on myself to fix it. But, in reality, it had *absolutely nothing to do with me*. So the things I felt and mental anguish I put on myself should have been avoided because it wasn't my fault. It wasn't me; it was them.

Now when things don't work out right away or even after months, I just move on. I let...it...go. Because it's probably much better anyway that these businesses or people don't become BrEpic clients. It would have been more hassle than it was worth.

My "disingenuous meter" is pretty accurate these days when meeting people, and here are some **tips I've learned that are clear red flags for the wrong type of client**.

01. They talk endlessly and don't listen to you or care about anything you have to say. Or they never ask you questions.
02. They bring up money or cost constantly.
03. They go into grand plans about their dreams without giving any reason why they will be able achieve anything.
04. They are referrals from other disingenuous people.
05. They practically beg you to work with them and try to nickel and dime you during negotiations.
06. They don't respect your time by showing up late or calling in late to initial meetings and then not apologizing.

It has taken me years – *years* – to whittle out almost all of these bad eggs. Some creep around every now and then.

If it helps, Entrepreneur's article titled "9 Telltale Signs You're Dealing With an Inauthentic Person" has some really great advice about toxic people. It notes that inauthentic folks are "generally full of themselves," "are manipulative and judgmental," "lack consistency," and "aren't interested in learning from their mistakes."

The last statement there is especially critical. The best entrepreneurs fail horribly but *then learn from those errors.* For every big success BrEpic has had, there have been dozens of failures before it. **Many times, failure is actually the best thing that can happen to you in the long run.** Remember, the only reason I have a company is because my journalist salary was cut in half and I couldn't find a job.

It's also more than OK to fire a client – and make sure the appropriate language is in your contracts. I've fired a few clients for not respecting my time (calling/emailing/texting at off hours) and having completely unrealistic expectations. Knock on wood, I've had only one client ever yell at me.

Forbes published a terrific article regarding "6 Reasons to Fire a Client." It says that clients who "show a basic lack of respect," others who "don't respond to you," or those that "are always slow to pay" should be canned.

We are only on this Earth for a short amount of time – watching my kids grow so quickly has only reinforced that – and the last thing I want to deal with is bad people. The business world is full of them, and I hope this chapter helps you eliminate those type of situations. That way, you can say "yes" to more of the right types of clients.

EPIC TAKEAWAYS:

1. People are people
2. People sometimes say they are interested and ready to move forward but don't follow through
3. When people don't follow through or say no, it's not personal...they just aren't ready and a right fit
4. Watch for red flags and just say no
5. Your time and talent are valuable; therefore, select your clients wisely

LINKS:

https://www.entrepreneur.com/article/313268

https://www.forbes.com/sites/allbusiness/2014/05/06/6-reasons-to-fire-a-client/#63e73e6bc512

CHAPTER TWENTY-THREE

BUILDING RELATIONSHIPS IS A LOT LIKE FARMING BECAUSE IT'S ABOUT PLANTING SEEDS AND WAITING FOR THINGS TO GROW

In late 2017, I had a nice breakfast with the owner of a giant international PR firm.

I just wanted to meet him to learn how he had grown a business, and there was no intent to gain business from it. I thanked him for his time and didn't hear from him again.

That was until late 2019, when he sent me an introductory email to a potential client – the CEO of an organic food company based in Texas. In the intro, he said he had been following my progress via social media for the last two years, and that my firm would be the perfect fit to tell this CEO's story to the masses. As of deadline for this manuscript, I'm still in negotiations with this businesswoman in Texas, but the point is still clear: **Business and relationships sometimes take a *long* time to develop.**

A brilliant attorney from California named Mark explained this idea perfectly when he spoke at a Chicago-based ProVisors meeting in 2019. Mark is one of the most connected people I know, and that's saying something. He is constantly making intros for people and connecting visionaries. And business always comes back to him. He is a networking master.

During his 30-minute talk to the group, Mark said something that was so clear and matter-of-fact that it is constantly ringing in my head. He stressed that **building relationships is a lot like farming because it's about planting seeds in people's heads and waiting for those seeds to grow. Those seeds inevitably will blossom into business when you're planting seeds with the right people.**

This mindset and idea have helped me so tremendously that I try to tell people about it when I first meet them. **It is crucial to think of business development as a long play and not something that happens overnight.**

Like farming, **it can take years for the right business relationships to develop**, the right mixture of timing, soil, patience and weather.

And **the more seeds you plant in the right people's heads, the more high-quality fruit (or business) is yielded!**

BrEpic is essentially one giant, worldwide farm of visionary people connecting with other visionary people. The company is a network of like-minded folks that enjoy talking to each other and love helping their businesses thrive and prosper.

Writing the above paragraph has been the best part of scribing this book. I was able to realize what my company truly is and what it will be moving forward!

And the beauty of BrEpic is there is **no limit** to how big this farm of amazing visionary crops can grow to!

When I connect with people, I always ask them what types of businesses could help them, whether it's attorneys, website builders, financial planners, event coordinators, graphic designers, marketers or anything else. And then I ask them to plant a seed in my head by telling me one critical thing I can remember about them, so when others ask for that particular thing, their name will immediately pop out.

I take tremendous joy when someone needs help getting on Wikipedia – and I actually know an expert in that field. Or whether someone needs a divorce attorney who charges between $200-$250 an hour, or one who has fees well over $500 an hour. Or if they require a Realtor who has properties in Mexico.

Like Mark, **I make intros every single day, and guess what happens in return? Organically, intros are made to me seemingly all the time – to the right group of people!**

I was a guest at a networking meeting in mid-2018 when I met a business coach named Lee. We didn't talk about our companies at all; instead we discussed how he lived and worked in Paris for years, and that I spoke a little French. Fast-forward 12 months, and Lee reached out to me because he was publishing a book and he wanted PR help to get the word out. **I hadn't spoken to him in a year, but had planted that seed with our Paris conversation. And it stuck.**

When you start a business, don't expect to have an instant giant crop of success. Instead, be patient and let those seeds grow. The harvest and re-harvesting from those seeds will be well worth the wait!

EPIC TAKEAWAYS:

1. Business relationships take time to grow
2. Growing business relationships is like farming and takes a willingness to plant seeds and giving them time to grow
3. The more seeds you plant, the more high-quality fruit you will grow
4. Plant seeds for those in your network too (share your powerful network of expert resources)
5. Introduce your community to high-quality experts and resources
6. The more high-quality introductions you do ... "you plant" ... the more high-quality introductions will come back to you.
7. The planting, allowing to grow, introducing, harvesting and re-harvesting will be well worth the wait

CHAPTER TWENTY-FOUR

DON'T TRY TO DO EVERYTHING YOURSELF. IT'S A RECIPE FOR FAILURE

Today is Jan. 1, 2020. It's a new day, new year, new decade. A moment to really think BIG!!

Five days from now, I will have started with a virtual assistant who will be helping me keep track of clients, schedule events and meetings, write and email contracts and invoices, and provide all sorts of other services.

It took me almost three years to get to this point: Where if BrEpic is going to be a truly global company – and it will be – that I have to start delegating more and more and more.

Slowly, but surely and strategically, I have scaled my company to bring on freelance reporters, a website designer and now a virtual assistant. This is just the start of the scaling process, and I can't wait to watch BrEpic expand.

In BrEpic's first year, I wasn't ready for this scaling effort. Even after two years, when I really understood how BrEpic's business model would work, I wasn't truly prepared to start adding bodies.

But now I am. It's time.

I've surrounded myself with numerous entrepreneurs who started as solopreneurs and then continued to think bigger and bigger and bigger. All of them told me that I had to eventually scale. For a long time, I resisted. **It's a huge mind change to work only _in_ the business as opposed to start working _on_ the business.** It's time for me to be able to work more and more on the business...to create a scalable structure that allows me to focus on the business instead of in the business.

In the first year, with the exception of filing my taxes, I did literally everything myself. I designed a website – it was NOT good. I networked, filled out invoices, wrote stories, pitched content to media, kept track of everything. It was overwhelming and many times I felt like I was just spinning my tires. I was worn down physically, but especially mentally.

Starting the second year, I found someone to build a far more respectable website. I also hired a videographer to create testimonials from clients at events. About 30 months in, I finally had others begin to write stories, while I still edited and pitched them.

I'm beyond thrilled to start partnering with a virtual assistant because this will allow me to spend far more time focusing on my Unique Ability to network with other visionaries and tell their stories. Remember, I could essentially do that all day, all night and never get tired of it. Besides spending time with my family, that is my true passion.

I also purchased a flip phone for weekend use. Only my wife has that number. **My personal assistant will monitor my emails and contact me only if it is a true emergency. So, I'll be taking a ton more "Free Days" as well. This will enable me to become even more laser-focused on how BrEpic will attract more high-end clients around the world.**

I possibly could have continued to be a one-man act, but the likely long-term result – as in a decade or two from now – would have been failure. **Constantly going at full throttle is not sustainable. It's not healthy, invigorating or manageable.**

This process of hiring a virtual assistant has been more than a year in the making. Switching from corporate to entrepreneur life required two full years in mental shift. Moving from essentially a solopreneur to running a "real" company has taken almost 12 more months.

I was talking to my personal coach in Strategic Coach, Amy, and she said I actually was extremely *fast* in making this transition. She said most entrepreneurs in my situation take much longer to start implementing the scaling process.

I started actively pursuing a virtual assistant in the third quarter of 2019. Many people have asked how I found the right one, and it of course came from a referral from an amazing visionary marketing entrepreneur in my network, Sonny. She raved about her virtual assistant, Suzanna, and said I had to talk to her.

I scheduled a call with Suzanna, who's based on the East Coast. Within 30 seconds, I knew I had discovered the right person. Suzanna was essentially answering my questions before I finished them. She *got* me. She enjoyed doing all the things that I did not like to do. I suggested the amount of time I thought I would need her each month, and she actually recommended even *less* hours because she wanted to slowly and strategically become a valued partner. Not only was this a relief to find Suzanna, but I was extremely thrilled to commence the process.

In the last few months, I've read up on the value of having a solid team behind me. Fast Company published an article – "4 Reasons You Shouldn't Try To Do Everything Yourself" – that has some incredible points. I believe the most important is that "nobody has ever actually done anything alone."

The paragraph states: *"In the history of our species, everyone who has ever accomplished anything has had parents or guardians who cared for them; educators, mentors, and role models who taught them essential skills; friends, supporters, and other interested parties who provided moral or intellectual or financial support; and countless partners who helped them build, tweak, promote, modify, expand, establish, and grow whatever it is that they ended up doing. To think otherwise is not only unhealthy, but it flies completely in the face of all human experience."*

Entrepreneur's article about "Transitioning From Solopreneur to a Team Leader" provided further explanation why I was prepared to make the next leap in my business. The story noted that entrepreneurs ready to build their supporting teams first had to master their own self-awareness.

"Self-awareness is the key to entrepreneurial success," the article said. *"For starters, it helps you realize your strengths and weaknesses. Knowing this allows you to surround yourself with the right people. Ideally, they complement your strengths and pick up the slack in your weaker areas."*

Now that I know my true strengths, and realize my weaknesses, I'm finding folks who can help take away everything I don't want to do and that I'm not exceptional at. Because **I want to be able to stay in my genius and provide exceptional and epic results.**

Being an entrepreneur has shown me my true potential. Adding a team behind me is going to allow BrEpic to reach even more of its full potential.

EPIC TAKEAWAYS:

1. You can't do it all alone and grow
2. In order to scale and sustain your growth you need a team to support you
3. You need to be able to have time to work on the business...not just in it
4. Build a team that supports you to work in your genius
5. Grow your business to its full potential

LINKS:

https://www.fastcompany.com/3029889/4-reasons-you-shouldnt-try-to-do-everything-yourself

https://www.entrepreneur.com/article/335357

CHAPTER TWENTY-FIVE

SOME OF THE BEST IDEAS COME DURING EARLY MORNING WORKOUTS OR RUNS

This book wouldn't have existed without a before-sunrise, freezing cold run in November.

I've been running six days a week outside, no matter the weather conditions, for more than 15 years. I started running to help alleviate the stress of a breakup 15 years ago, and I never stopped.

Some of the best ideas I've ever had – including writing this book – have popped into my head during these runs, which range from 3-5 miles. Again, there was never an intent to scribe this book. This list of 30 things I've learned from high-level entrepreneurs was supposed to be a simple social media post. But, during a super early morning jog around Thanksgiving, as I thought about all the great responses – including people begging me to write a book – I'm like, *I'll just do it!*

Of the thousands of business owners I know, I can think of only a handful who don't take care of themselves physically. **This life is too demanding if you don't have some type of workout release.** And in case it's not obvious, **regular exercise likely will improve your energy, memory, mental health and overall happiness.** As Healthline noted, "regular exercise offers incredible benefits that can improve nearly every aspect of your health from the inside out."

I literally don't think I could function without my runs. It is part of my very being. On Sundays, the one day I don't run, I am more irritable, impatient and antsy. It is a noticeable difference in demeanor. I eat a lot of food. If I didn't run routinely, I'd be extremely overweight.

The key for me is *starting* the day with a run. Usually, I wake up between 4:30-5 a.m., do a bit of planning work, and then leave the house – most of the time before the sun rises. On some days when I have morning networking meetings in Downtown Chicago, I'll set the alarm for 2 or 3 a.m. Some people may think that's over the top, but others who understand the value of a stress-release part of the day just get it.

I like running in the dark, especially when it's super cold, even icy. It's hard to see, so my other senses become more attuned to the surroundings. I also become incredibly focused on every step, never knowing if there's a skunk around the next turn (knock on wood, I've never been sprayed, but have come close a few times).

Before sunrise is also a great time to be alone with your thoughts. It's relaxing, and with the exception of the Muse, U2, Tool or some of my other favorite bands blasting in my ears, there are few other sounds.

It's peaceful.

Angie Fifer, an executive board member of the Association for Applied Sport Psychology, summed it up perfectly when she told Runners World regarding running in the dark: "No one is looking and judging, so in your mind you think, 'I can just go, without inhibitions.'"

When I'm running, I'm not distracted. I can come up with an idea and then spend 10-15 in my head figuring out whether it will work without an email or text or person interrupting me.

CEO Chase Garbarino provided another great point by explaining to Inc that the "sense of accomplishment first thing in the morning sets the tone for the rest of the workday."

Running keeps me focused, structured, healthy, optimistic, relaxed and in tune with the world around me. I also earn great sleep because I'm so tired by 8:30 or 9 p.m., that I conk right out and don't twist and turn when going to bed.

Virgin Airlines CEO Richard Branson <u>in a blog post</u> said regular exercise "puts me in a great mind frame to get down to business, and also helps me to get the rest I need each night."

There's nothing more satisfying than knowing I have applied myself both physically and mentally every day," Branson said.

If you don't work out regularly, I hope you read this chapter and begin to incorporate exercise into your day. Try out different types of exercise and find the one that works for you. If you haven't tried running before the rooster starts crowing, give it a shot. I think you'll really find it rewarding in countless ways.

EPIC TAKEAWAYS:

1. Life is demanding; therefore, it is important to have a regular workout for stress release and your health
2. Exercise allows us to avoid distraction and let the ideas flow
3. Starting the day with exercise sets a powerful and positive tone for the day
4. Exercising in the morning can help you sleep better at night

LINKS:

https://www.healthline.com/nutrition/10-benefits-of-exercise#section11

https://www.runnersworld.com/training/a20865874/running-faster-at-night/

https://www.inc.com/john-brandon/8-entrepreneurs-share-their-morning-workout-routine.html

https://www.virgin.com/richard-branson/whats-health-your-success

CHAPTER TWENTY-SIX

THE FEELING OF HEARING ONE YES FAR OUTWEIGHS THE FEELING OF HEARING 20 NO'S

One of my clients recently posted a Forbes article on LinkedIn that revealed how Walt Disney was rejected 300 times by bankers and financiers before finding backing for Disney World.

But Disney, like all the great entrepreneurs, never gave up. Disney World didn't open until five years after his death, but look at what his determination led to.

I went to the movie theater in 2016 to watch "The Founder," the film about McDonald's tycoon Ray Kroc played brilliantly by Michael Keaton. There's a scene early in the movie where Keaton stares coldly toward the ceiling while lying on his back in bed – an absolute deadlock drive to succeed. I'm routinely reminded of this part of the film when dealing with rejection and always pushing through it.

God knows how many times Kroc was told No before he started hearing Yes on his mission to franchise McDonald's around the world. What I do understand is that if you are an entrepreneur, you will be turned down, scoffed at, brushed aside, ignored, rejected, laughed at, denied and doubted more than you can ever possibly fathom.

Entrepreneurs are survivors because they simply never quit, no matter how many shots they take in the stomach. Think of the beatings Rocky Balboa took in every movie, and then apply it to how your brain and well-being might feel after getting pulverized time after time after time.

Many of my clients have been through immense trauma, either through rough upbringings or tragedies in their lives, but, unlike many, they found a way to not only handle those events, but thrive in spite of them.

There is no doubt that the deaths of my father and brother, breakups from ex-girlfriends, failed job interviews, my pay cut at DNAinfo and all sorts of other disasters prepared me for being an entrepreneur. Almost everything great that has happened in my life – from meeting my wife to starting a business – has followed massive rejections.

What keeps me going – besides having a wonderful family, great work-life balance, awesome clients, a thriving business, a huge network of visionary thinkers and basically the freedom to do whatever I want – is the search for the right "Yes" from the right person.

If 20 No's lead to 1 Yes to the perfect-fit client, that's fine by me. Because I know that person will almost certainly refer me to potential clients who are just like them. And that only increases my closing rate and long-term vision to make BrEpic a global brand partnering with the best organizations on the planet.

Dr. Sean Wise, a professor of entrepreneurship and a seed stage founder, told Huffington Post that **entrepreneurs should not only accept, but *embrace*, failing.**

"There are literally thousands of stories of both large and small companies facing rejection in one form or another – only to preserve and win," Wise said, adding that starting a business

"*is a marathon not a sprint.* **The goal is success but the road will be long and full of bumps along the way.**"

I've realized that No's, while sometimes deflating and annoying, happen for a reason. **Either the person is nickel and dime, they're not visionaries, they're not ready for a giant media push, they're placing their resources elsewhere or it's just timing.** Looking back on the thousands of No's, I'm glad almost all of them didn't lead to client relationships.

The No's have helped me sharpen my sales pitch, discover the perfect clients, strengthen BrEpic's business model and so much more.

I am so honored when someone or a business says Yes to working with BrEpic. The thrill – the rush!!! – of realizing that someone is paying you great money to do what you love while appreciating and valuing your work is something I can't describe unless you've felt it yourself.

I've never dug for gold, but I imagine it's like sifting through mountains of dirt before discovering a big-ole nugget.

Everyone I work with now is exceptional because only outstanding people will say Yes to what I offer and how I offer it. The No's also have helped me eliminate other potential bad fits.

If I can stress one point, it's that hearing No is a *good* thing. Even if it takes thousands of rejections, **if you don't quit, you will find the right people to say Yes!**

EPIC TAKEAWAYS:

1. Entrepreneurs are survivors that have determination and commitment to their vision
2. "No's" are OK, they just aren't the right fit
3. You want to look for the right fit
4. "No's" help you fine tune your offering, style, sales conversation and approach.
5. Persevere. Don't quit and find the right "yes" client for you and your company

LINKS:

https://www-forbes-com.cdn.ampproject.org/c/s/www.forbes.com/sites/jamesasquith/2020/12/29/did-you-know-walt-disney-was-rejected-300-times-for-mickey-mouse-and-his-theme-park/amp/

https://www.huffpost.com/entry/dealing-with-entrepreneurial-rejection_b_59dcc451e4b0a1bb90b830ed

CHAPTER TWENTY-SEVEN

CONFIDENCE IS A GREAT THING AND AN AWESOME ATTRACTOR TO OTHER CONFIDENT PEOPLE

I routinely tell people that I'm extremely good at running BrEpic, an awesome father and husband, and pretty much useless to society besides that.

I usually get a laugh when I say that, but really, I'm not kidding.

I know that BrEpic provides a superior service and is worth every bit of the investment. I also understand that what my firm does and the results it obtains for clients only appeals to visionaries like me because we think the same way and cherish partnering with only the best of the best people.

I can go into a room with 20 people for a presentation, and **I am so confident in my abilities that I will almost immediately weed out all non-visionaries and draw the attention of only the cream-of-the-crop business owners.**

Supreme confidence can rub many people the wrong way, but those people won't be my clients anyway. The ones I want to team with almost always have the same self-confidence that I do because they have also built super successful businesses *... by ... being ... confident!*

Confidence according to the Oxford Dictionary is "a feeling of self-assurance arising from one's appreciation of one's own abilities or qualities."

This is MUCH different than cockiness, which is described as "someone who is very arrogant and assumes they know all the answers," according to Your Dictionary.

I can't stand cocky people, who think they know everything and don't understand their limitations. I'll never work with those people because they think they're always right and don't realize when they're wrong.

Confidence allows entrepreneurs to raise the rates, grow their businesses, *and identify and appreciate others* who can help them achieve their goals.

I've learned you can't fake confidence. You either have it or you don't. I've been around my fair share of BS artists who talk a lot and deliver little. They dodge questions and lack directness. They don't say what they actually *do*.

My fraternity brother and great friend Andrew is an exceptional financial entrepreneur based in Minnesota. He started his entrepreneurial journey shortly after graduating college and has been on a massive upward trajectory ever since. He is extremely confident in his abilities and also has built a great team around him while purchasing a new gleaming office building in the last year. He is one of the nicest people I know, and there is nothing cocky about him.

Andy and I talk about once a week, and when it's not to discuss fantasy football, it's to rejoice about our respective businesses. He always has great advice to share, especially when describing how confidence leads to generating business and new clients.

I think his best point was when he said that prospective clients know they're dealing with a confident entrepreneur when it's obvious that entrepreneur doesn't need their money.

I obviously want financial gain, but not if it's from the wrong person who isn't a visionary or running an exceptional business. I'm more than comfortable saying no. Because of BrEpic's success and my directness, I don't need to have a bunch of new clients constantly signing up. **I only want to partner with the greatest entrepreneurs out there. I have confidence to decline or not chase the wrong fit for my business.**

I recently perused a piece from Lifehack titled "How to Be Confident Without Being Cocky." It's a fun, quick read with a plethora of nuggets.

For example:

"If you scoff at the notion that you have any limitations, you need more than ever to realize that you do. Everyone sucks as something. In fact, everyone sucks at most things. The thing is that we need to know which ones they are to avoid the 'Superman Syndrome' or the idea that everything you do or can do you are instantly good at."

A story from Life Coach Directory titled "Why is self-confidence and self-belief so important to a business owner?" had four crucial points about confident entrepreneurs that I strongly endorse:

1. **Confident business owners are willing to put in the time and energy** *to educate themselves on marketing, leadership skills, effective listening skills, building their own personal brand and developing executive presence so they are seen as someone who is assertive and creative.*

2. **They are fearless and have a heightened sense of self-awareness** so they know their own blind spots and shortcomings and are willing to make changes within themselves to excel in their business.
3. **Confident business owners know that,** in order to successfully deal with clients, plan strategies, execute policies and make influential decisions, **they need to portray their confidence. This helps in encouraging people to trust them,** value their opinions and rely on their judgement.
4. **Confident business owners know that hiring a business coach can help them build even more confidence.** Coaching can challenge how they see their business and design a powerful vision for their business by combining imagination with action. This supports them in becoming great at what they do – after all, developing flexibility and confidence must be designed, rehearsed and constantly cultivated.

My superpowers are writing and pitching viral stories, and connecting with high-level entrepreneurs. I'm also a really good dad and pretty decent husband.

I know that I have countless limitations. I'm confident enough that I realize others can – and will – help me with everything else. What are your superpowers?

EPIC TAKEAWAYS:

1. Confidence in yourself, business and what you bring to clients is critical to the success of your business
2. Confidence is different than cockiness (over-confident in everything)
3. Don't chase clients; Confident entrepreneurs don't need "that sale"
4. Confident business owners are willing to put in the time and energy needed to achieve their goals
5. Know your superpowers and have confidence to bring them forward

LINKS:

https://www.lifehack.org/articles/lifehack/how-to-be-confident-without-being-cocky.html

https://www.lifecoach-directory.org.uk/memberarticles/why-is-confidence-so-important-as-a-business-owner

CHAPTER TWENTY-EIGHT

MAKING MORE MONEY DOESN'T EQUATE TO MORE HAPPINESS

In 2018, I had almost quadrupled the most yearly income I had ever made as a journalist.

And I also had never been more miserable.

If you think earning more money than you ever thought possible will lead to more happiness than you've ever dreamt of, think again.

I learned that more money can lead to more bills, more stress and more pressure to try and make even more money.

Cash is definitely not a substitute for joy.

Tony Robbins told CNBC about the downside of making more money, noting **that people obsess over "only making money instead of on improving quality of life for themselves and the people they care about."**

"Really, quality of life comes by finding a way to add more value to other people's lives," Robbins said.

As I discussed in Chapter 11, my main issue during my darkest days was waiting for potential and current clients to sign contracts and looking too far in advance to months where

I had no income slotted. The thought of banking $30,000, $40,000 or $50,000 in one month and then not knowing when the next paycheck would come from a few months down the road was paralyzing.

For months, it was hard to get any good sleep, even though I was financially just fine.

The quest for more, more, more had given me so much *less* than I had anticipated. Instead of focusing on my family, helping others and my health, I had placed almost everything on finding new clients and new sources of income.

It was a hopeless plunge to the bottom.

Talking to my wife, my therapist and those close to me in my network certainly saved me and provided the answers I needed. **I started to figure out what really mattered – and what would lead to true happiness.**

In a Forbes piece called "**When Money Doesn't Equal Happiness**," there's a passage from Tony Hsieh, who sold LinkExchange to Microsoft for $265 million. Hsieh said the huge amount of wealth didn't add to his overall happiness in the least.

"I thought about how easily we are all brainwashed by our society and culture to stop thinking and just assume by default that more money equals more success and more happiness, when ultimately happiness is really just about enjoying life. ... I didn't realize it at the time, but it was a turning point for me in my life. I had decided to stop chasing the money, and start chasing the passion," Hsieh said.

Now I spend most of my time chasing the passion, whether that's super-awesome experiences with my family – or just chilling out at home – or interacting with some of the coolest entrepreneurs on the planet. Very few of the conversations I have with visionaries revolves around work; they really focus on living life to the fullest.

I find great happiness in helping others, or connecting them with other wonderful people. There is immense joy when you get someone a job or help them land an interview, or introduce them to someone who changes their life in dramatic ways. Those are feelings that never go away or never grow old.

I need to be clear that having money is not bad. It allows me to do fun things like get better tickets to concerts, games or shows. I fly first class now for work trips because that's where potential BrEpic clients likely sit as well. If my family wants to go to on a fun trip – like shark fishing in the Florida Keys – I don't think twice about booking it.

So how much money do you really need to be happy?

Purdue University in 2018 released a study that forecasted the optimal point of how much money it takes to make an individual happy.

"It's been debated at what point does money no longer change your level of well-being," Andrew T. Jebb, the lead author and doctoral student in Purdue's Department of Psychological Sciences said in the report. "We found that the ideal income point is $95,000 for life evaluation and $60,000 to $75,000 for emotional well-being. Again, this amount is for individuals and would likely be higher for families."

What was most interesting was "the study also found once the threshold was reached, further increases in income tended to be associated with **reduced life satisfaction and a lower level of well-being**."

When I first started BrEpic, I was overjoyed that I was already making more than I ever had as a journalist. About a year into the business, I met with a terrific financial entrepreneur named Lloyd who had come from extreme poverty growing up on Chicago's West Side to running a billion-dollar investment business. During our conversation and knowing the results BrEpic was producing, he said I was going to make a *lot* of money. That shocked me, but it didn't make me happy. In fact, like the Purdue study discussed, the more I made did *not* result in more overall satisfaction.

If you believe a windfall of money is going to solve your problems, reduce stress or lead to this previously unknown happiness, you're probably dead wrong. I had to learn the hard way. I hope during your entrepreneurial journey that you don't make the same mistake. At a certain point, money is just money. Make sure to spend time getting clear on what truly makes you happy and do those things.

EPIC TAKEAWAYS:

1. More money doesn't equal happiness
2. More money is just more money, and can actually add pressure and stress
3. Take time to find out what makes you happy and build that into your life
4. Choose to build a life that is meaningful to you

LINKS:

https://www.cnbc.com/2019/03/28/tony-robbins-money-isnt-the-source-of-lasting-happiness.html

https://www.forbes.com/sites/brockblake/2014/02/21/when-money-doesnt-equal-happiness/#6a02e69540e2

https://www.purdue.edu/newsroom/releases/2018/Q1/money-only-buys-happiness-for-a-certain-amount.html

BEING LUCKY IS PART OF SUCCESS, BUT YOU HAVE TO PUT YOURSELF IN THE POSITION TO BE LUCKY

I subscribe to the belief that if you're on time to a meeting, you're actually 15 minutes late.

Arriving even a second after a scheduled meeting time is completely unacceptable to me, so I plan accordingly. I try to arrive at or near the meeting location way, way, way ahead of time and just work from a coffeeshop or restaurant in the area.

This was the case during one of my frequent Downtown Chicago meetings in the summer of 2019. I had arrived well over an hour early and was at an intersection with Dunkin' Donuts and a Starbucks on opposing corners. I decided to go to the Dunkin' Donuts for no apparent reason.

As I sat down and set up shop, I noticed one of my networking friends. He's a great guy named Kit, and he owns a financial planning business. After plugging in, I walked over to say hello to Kit and the person he was sitting with, a marketer named Mike. Kit then explained to Mike that the online educational software company for which he worked could be a perfect client for my firm.

Mike and I traded business cards, and a few weeks later, we had a meeting at his office. He was impressed, so I sent him a contract. And while we haven't finalized a deal yet, in the ensuing weeks, Mike introduced me to one of his networking connections, William, the CEO of a major allergy-free food company, and he quickly did become my firm's client to the tune of a great five-figure deal.

Of course, luck played a part in this. I could have gone to Starbucks, and I probably never would have met Mike, who then would have never set me up with William.

But I choose to look at this event as *making my own luck.*

If I hadn't put in years of effort trying to meet the right people, then signing up for the right networking groups, then actually talking to people and becoming their friends, and then taking time to stop working on my laptop to get up and approach Kit during his meeting with Mike, there would have never been the chance to earn a five-figure contract.

I had put myself in a position to be lucky.

It's the same situation when Allstate signed with my firm even though they initially didn't even know I had a business. As a reminder, Allstate reached out to me to be a judge in a contest that showcased inspirational teens because I had a lengthy portfolio of writing about amazing teens and young adults, and I had a fairly large social media following. Allstate considered me an influencer.

If I hadn't answered Allstate's original email or hadn't built up my social media network into the tens of thousands or written all these stories about incredible people, I would have never had that first meeting with Allstate.

Obviously, it was lucky to partner with one of the country's most well-known organizations at the start of BrEpic's journey, but the previous 20-plus years of journalism work had put me in a place to be lucky.

Entrepreneur's article about "10 Proven Ways to Make Your Own Luck" has some perfect ideas like "be social and improve your odds," "help others and find out how lucky you are," "be on the lookout for luck," and "create your own luck through hard work."

"You can thus create your own luck by being aware of your circumstances and surroundings. By simply noticing and acting on opportunities or listening to your hunches, you allow more luck into your life," the article states.

So many of the topics I've detailed in previous chapters have led to a mammoth amount of "lucky" situations for my company that have resulted in big deals.

I feel extremely lucky to run such an awesome company, but I also know I've laid the foundation for that luck to pay off!

EPIC TAKEAWAYS:

1. Set yourself up for success
2. Create space in your schedule to be open to opportunities
3. Lay a strong foundation that you can build off of
4. Be aware of circumstances and opportunities and be willing to step forward and create your own connection and luck
5. Follow your hunches and intuition

LINK:

https://www.entrepreneur.com/article/286336

CHAPTER THIRTY

IF YOU HAVE A CLEAR VISION FOR A BIGGER AND BRIGHTER FUTURE, IT WILL HAPPEN

I'm 35,000 feet in the air right now, sitting in first class on my way to meet a visionary new client from Utah who runs a multi-million-dollar business from her home.

Years ago in the corporate world – or even when I began BrEpic – I never could have believed in my wildest dreams that this scenario would have been possible.

Now it's just reality – and only the *beginning* of this epic adventure.

Dan Sullivan, who founded Strategic Coach and is a true genius, tells entrepreneurs all the time that it's imperative that to achieve unprecedented success, that they must envision a bigger and brighter future. As Inc. noted in a piece about having a vision for your life, Sullivan stressed: *"Surround yourself with people who remind you more of your future than of your past."*

His advice is essential. **It's the most important thing to build momentum, have that go-for-it attitude and actually make it happen!!!** If someone doesn't embrace or support my vision, that's on them. I only surround myself with people who get it!

I have written down my life goals, which include living to at least 100 years old. I also plan to swim with great white sharks, see the polar bears in Svalbard, go to Alaska with my family for a month and attend my grandchildren's weddings. The last goal is by far the most important. Remember, family comes first. Without that foundation, none of this success means anything.

My mind, just as it has guided BrEpic on its current spike, will lead the company to better and better heights. Not only do I believe this will happen ... I KNOW IT WILL HAPPEN!

There is no doubt that this book will help countless people change their lives and businesses for the better. I have implemented the advice from the great entrepreneurs highlighted in the previous chapters and completely altered my life, my expectations for life, my capacity to build wealth, a network and friendships, and my ability to assist others in realizing their dreams can come true, too!

I thank God every single day that my salary was cut in half on that fateful Feb. 10, 2017. That setback allowed me to discover a career and destiny I never thought imaginable.

The entrepreneur life is not for everyone, especially those that can't plow through overwhelming failure or rejection. Again, I need to be clear that if you become an entrepreneur, you always certainly become depressed at one time or another. But you can conquer it!

Thousands of people have influenced me on my entrepreneurial path. I am forever thankful to them and will always pay it forward.

If you ask me for help, I will help you. If you have any questions about the details in this book, please don't hesitate to reach out.

Everyone has epic potential. I hope this book helps you reach it!

EPIC TAKEAWAYS:

1. A clear vision of your bigger and brighter future is key to your success
2. Go for it! Be all in and committed to bringing your vision forward
3. Believe in yourself, your vision and your future
4. If you need/want help...remember to reach out!
5. You have EPIC Potential! Go for it!

LINK:

https://www.inc.com/benjamin-p-hardy/do-you-have-a-3-year-vision-for-your-life.html

ABOUT THE AUTHOR

Justin Breen is the founder and CEO of BrEpic Communications LLC, a PR firm that works exclusively with visionaries and exceptional businesses around the world.

BrEpic has partnered with incredible brands, including Allstate, University of Illinois, Morgan Stanley, Salvation Army, White Lodging, Burwood Group, Schuler Scholar Program, Cultivate Advisors, LISC, The Safe + Fair Company, The Chicago Academy for the Arts, Alverno Laboratories, McCormick Foundation, and numerous other companies, CEOs, entrepreneurs, attorneys, healthcare professionals and remarkable individuals.

Breen is hard-wired to seek out and create viral, thought-provoking stories that the media craves, and he finds the best stories when he networks with visionary entrepreneurs and executives who understand the value of investing in themselves and their businesses. Breen has built an international network of extraordinary people and believes strongly in the power of introductions and creating important relationships through those introductions.

A Northbrook, Illinois, native, Breen earned a full academic scholarship to the University of Illinois at Urbana-Champaign, where he graduated with a degree in News-Editorial Journalism and has served as the longtime Journalism Chair for the College of Media Alumni Board.

Breen is involved in numerous high-level entrepreneurial groups, including Strategic Coach, The Entrepreneurs' Organization Accelerator Program and ProVisors.

Breen lives in Glenview, Illinois, with his wife, Dr. Sarah Breen – a pediatrician – and their two awesome sons, Jake and Chase.

Breen can be reached at Justin@BrEpicLLC.com and www.BrEpicLLC.com.

His social media handles include
- https://www.facebook.com/BrEpic/
- https://twitter.com/BrEpicBreen
- https://www.instagram.com/brepicbreen/
- https://www.linkedin.com/in/justinbreen1/

REVIEWS

Luminous . . . **Justin packs 5,000 watts into this must-read book for anyone who wants to amplify their business or life. Read it now . . . and then—read it again**. It's packed with inspiration, ideas and intelligence.
> **Matt Toledo - CEO, ProVisors**

Practical yet personal, Justin Breen's book offers advice that appeals to the common sensibilities of anybody who reads it. Justin establishes a strong tone by poignantly describing how the impact of the deaths of his father and younger brother affected his career path, relatable experiences for every professional. His use of anecdotes make you think as much as they make you smile and drive home their desired point. Yes, tweeting at McDonald's about putting the Extra Value Meal back on the menu really did lead to a new client who learned about Justin's cheeseburger obsession on Facebook. From fun stories to firm directives, it's all there for readers to consider in smart, succinct chapters that make this an easy read.
> **David Haugh**
> **Longtime Chicago columnist and radio host**
> **670TheScore.com**

When his career in journalism came to an abrupt halt, author Justin Breen found himself at the forefront of a frightening new beginning. Instead of allowing himself to be paralyzed by fear of the unknown, he put one foot in front of the other and trusted in what he knew best from his decades as a journalist. He knew the newsworthy content he truly enjoyed writing, and now he was going to take it and maximize it for clients professionally. He set out to accomplish this without sacrificing the most important content of his life—his wife and two young sons.

Chapter by chapter, this book delves into Justin's real-life stories of how his decision-making was influenced, and also fueled, by very particular over-arching principles that every entrepreneur would benefit from. He breaks down profound steps he has learned along the way that took his business from infancy to an international success. Justin illustrates how taking effective action by implementing these key concepts guided him through obstacles to find unimaginable opportunities.

    Kristin Barnette McCarthy, Trial Attorney at Kralovec, Jambois & Schwartz

Epic Business by Justin Breen **is a must-read! He is one of the great geniuses of our time.** Discover his story and success secrets in this book.

    Sarah Victory, Award-winning speaker, best-selling author

This book is truly inspirational and shares some of the similar experiences I faced as an employee transitioning into the entrepreneurial world. It can be lonely at times, but with the right system and network, you will thrive as an entrepreneur. **If you're interested in becoming an entrepreneur or taking your business to the next level, this is the book to read.** Great job, Justin!

    Jeff Badu, CPA
    CEO, Badu Enterprises, LLC

Justin has created a book that is captivating, compelling, sincere, real and raw, and in parts, funny. **Justin draws you into the book in such a way that, personally, I could not put it down and actually finished it in one day, which is something I never do with non-fiction books of this type.** I knew that I would go back into the book and reread the 30 chapters to glean all the rich wisdom of his journey from the birth of BrEpic to the massively successful company that it is today. This book is truly insightful and engaging for us all.

Linda F. Patten, Leadership Trainer for Women Entrepreneurs and Changemakers – President &CEO, Dare2Lead With Linda

Epic Business is not just a book on business, it is a book that walks you through the steps of doubling-down on what you are good at while staying true to your passions in life.
When reading *Epic Business*, you might remember that old adage, "know how to made God laugh? Tell him your plans." In this combination memoir and business book, Justin walks you through what could have been one of the worst events in his career. It's a journey to find a life much bigger. He shares a parable-like story providing 30 specific lessons like, *Don't Try Everything Yourself*, *Never Stop Learning*, and *Learn from Tough Times*. He provides epic takeaways; the whole book is direct, succinct and full of gold. Bonus: follow the links that Justin provides to augment your learning. Priceless.

Jeanne Alford, Alford Communications

Are you motivated to significantly grow your business AND to have the freedom to live the life you want? Look no further than this book, it is your go-to guide! **Epic Business by Justin Breen is a powerful resource that is packed with effective secrets that you can implement immediately.** Breen has extensive journalism and leadership experience and he highlights straight-forward, compelling strategies that will truly help everyone who reads this book. With *Epic Business* by your side, you are making the life-changing choice to guide your business and your life to become even more epic!

Wendy K. Benson, MBA, OTR/L and Elizabeth A. Myers, RN
Co-Authors, The Confident Patient
2x2 Health: Private Health Concierge

Epic Business by Justin Breen is an extremely powerful resource for new or seasoned entrepreneurs. Especially In today's uncertain and fast-paced time, it is a great tool to accelerate your business. Justin is open, honest and authentic in sharing his personal journey-trials, tribulations and success. I loved that in the very beginning Justin talks about prioritizing family over work and to lead with your values. This is a great reminder of the very reason one chooses the entrepreneurial direction but forgets along the way. **Although I have been an entrepreneur myself for 20 years, I picked up some new insights that I could apply in my business.**

Seema Giri, PMP

Award Winning Author, International Speaker, Anthology Compiler and Holistic Lifestyle Strategist

Made in the USA
San Bernardino, CA
11 August 2020